Your Five Gallants by Thomas Middleton

Thomas Middleton was born in London in April 1580 and baptised on 18th April.

Middleton was aged only five when his father died. His mother remarried but this unfortunately fell apart into a fifteen year legal dispute regarding the inheritance due Thomas and his younger sister.

By the time he left Oxford, at the turn of the Century, Middleton had and published Microcynicon: Six Snarling Satirese which was denounced by the Archbishop of Canterbury and publicly burned.

In the early years of the 17th century, Middleton wrote topical pamphlets. One – Penniless Parliament of Threadbare Poets was reprinted several times and the subject of a parliamentary inquiry.

These early years writing plays continued to attract controversy. His writing partnership with Thomas Dekker brought him into conflict with Ben Jonson and George Chapman in the so-called War of the Theatres.

His finest work with Dekker was undoubtedly The Roaring Girl, a biography of the notorious Mary Frith.

In the 1610s, Middleton began another playwriting partnership, this time with the actor William Rowley, producing another slew of plays including Wit at Several Weapons and A Fair Quarrel.

The ever adaptable Middleton seemed at ease working with others or by himself. His solo writing credits include the comic masterpiece, A Chaste Maid in Cheapside, in 1613.

In 1620 he was officially appointed as chronologer of the City of London, a post he held until his death.

The 1620s saw the production of his and Rowley's tragedy, and continual favourite, The Changeling, and of several other tragicomedies.

However in 1624, he reached a peak of notoriety when his dramatic allegory A Game at Chess was staged by the King's Men. Though Middleton's approach was strongly patriotic, the Privy Council silenced the play after only nine performances at the Globe theatre, having received a complaint from the Spanish ambassador.

What happened next is a mystery. It is the last play recorded as having being written by Middleton.

Thomas Middleton died at his home at Newington Butts in Southwark in the summer of 1627, and was buried on July 4th, in St Mary's churchyard which today survives as a public park in Elephant and Castle.

Index of Contents
Dramatis Personae
Induction
ACT I

Scene I - A Room in Frippery's House
Scene Ii - A Room in Katherine's House
ACT II
Scene I - A Room in Primero's House
Scene II - A Street
Scene III - A Room in Primero's House
Scene IV - A Room in the Mitre
ACT III
Scene I - A Room in Tailby's lodging
Scene II - Combe Park
Scene III - Near Combe Park
Scene IV - A Street
Scene V - A Room in Primero's House
ACT IV
Scene I - Before Tailby's Lodging
Scene II - A Hall in Tailby's Lodging
Scene III - A Room with a Door Opening into Fitsgrave's Chamber
Scene IV - A Street
Scene V - Another Street
Scene VI - The Middle Aisle of St. Paul's
Scene VII - A Room in Mistress Newcut's House
Scene IV - A Street
ACT V
Scene I - A Chamber
Scene II - A Hall in Katherine's House
Thomas Middleton – A Short Biography
Thomas Middleton – A Concise Bibliography

Dramatis Personae
FRIPPERY, the broker-gallant
PRIMERO, the bawd-gallant
Justinian GOLDSTONE, the cheating-gallant
PURSENET, the pocket-gallant
TAILBY, the whore-gallant
FITSGRAVE, a gentleman
BUNGLER, cousin to Mistress Newcut
PYAMONT
ARTHUR, servant to Frippery
FULK, servant to Goldstone
BOY, servant to Pursenet
JACK, servant to Tailby
MARMADUKE, servant to Mistress Newcut
Two FELLOWS
Jeronimo Bedlam, a SERVANT friendly to Fitsgrave
A SERVANT of the Mitre
VINTNER, named Jack

Two DRAWERS
Two GENTLEMEN
TAILOR
SERVANTS to Mistresses Cleveland, Newbold, and Tiffany]
Two CONSTABLES
PAINTER]
KATHERINE, a wealthy orphan
MISTRESS NEWCUT, a merchant's wife
NOVICE
Three COURTESANS

INDUCTION

PRESENTER, or Prologue, passing over the stage; the bawd-gallant **PRIMERO**, with three wenches gallantly attired, meets him; the whore-gallant **TAILBY**, the pocket-gallant **PURSENET**, the cheating-gallant **GOLDSTONE**, kiss these three wenches, and depart in a little whisper and wanton action. Now, for the other, the broker-gallant **FRIPPERY**, he sits at home yet, I warrant you, at this time of day, summing up his pawns. Hactenus quasi inductio, a little glimpse giving.

ACT I

SCENE I - A Room in Frippery's House.

FRIPPERY discovered summing up his pawns, one **FELLOW** standing by him. Enter a **SECOND FELLOW** led in by **ARTHUR**.

ARTHUR
Is your pawn good and sound, sir?

SECOND FELLOW
I'll pawn my life for that, sir.

ARTHUR
Place yourself there then; I will seek to prefer it presently. My master is very jealous of the pestilence; marry, the pox sits at meat and meal with him.

[**SECOND FELLOW** retires.

FRIPPERY [Reads]
"Lent the fifth day of September to Mistress Onset upon her gown and taffeta petticoat with three broad silver laces, three pound fifteen shillings. Lent to Justice Cropshin upon both his velvet jackets, five pound ten shillings. Lent privately to my Lady Newcut upon her gilt casting-bottle and her silver lie-pot, fifty-five shillings."

ARTHUR

Sir—

FRIPPERY [Reads]
"Lent to Sir Oliver Needy upon his taffeta cloak, beaver hat, and perfumed leather-jerkin, six pound five shillings."

ARTHUR
May it please your worship—

FRIPPERY [Reads]
"Lent to Master Andrew Lucifer upon his flame-coloured doublet and blue taffeta hose"—Top the candle, sirrah; methinks the light burns blue: when came that suit in?

ARTHUR
'T'as lain above the year now.

FRIPPERY
Fire and brimstone! Cut it out into matches; the white linings will serve for tinder.

ARTHUR
And with little help, sir; they are almost black enough already. Sir, here's another come with a pawn.

FRIPPERY
Keep him aside awhile, and reach me hither the bill of the last week.

ARTHUR
'Tis here at hand, sir.

FRIPPERY
Now, sir, what's your pawn?

FIRST FELLOW
The second part of a gentlewoman's gown, sir; the lower half, I mean.

FRIPPERY
I apprehend you easily, the breeches of the gown.

FIRST FELLOW
Very proper, for she wears the doublet at home; a guest that lies in my house, sir; she looks every hour for her cousin out a' th' country.

FRIPPERY
O, her cousin lies here; 'a may mistake in that. My friend, of what parish is your pawn?

FIRST FELLOW
Parish? Why, Saint Clement's, sir.

FRIPPERY [To **SECOND FELLOW**]

I'll come to you presently. [To **FIRST FELLOW**] What parish is your pawn, my friend? [Reads] "Saint Bride's, five; Saint Dunstan's, none; Saint Clement's, three." Three at Clement's? Away with your pawn, sir, your parish is infected! I will neither purchase the plague for sixpence in the pound and a groat bill-money, nor venture my small stock into contagious parishes: you have your answer; fare you well, as fast as you can, sir.

FIRST FELLOW
The pox arrest you, sir, at the suit of the suburbs!

FRIPPERY
Ay, welcome, welcome.

FIRST FELLOW
For, I think, plague scorns your company.

[Exit.

FRIPPERY
I rank with chief gallants; I love to smell safely. [Reads] "Lent in the vacation to Master Proctor upon his spiritual gown five angels, and upon his corporal doublet fifteen shillings; sum, three pound five shillings."

ARTHUR
Sir—

FRIPPERY
Now, sir?

ARTHUR [Bringing forward a trunk]
Here's one come in with a trunk of apparel.

FRIPPERY
Whence comes it?

ARTHUR
From Saint Martin's-in-the-Field.

FRIPPERY
Saint Martin's-in-the-Field? [Reads] "Saint Mary Maudlin, two; Saint Martin's, none." Here's an honest fellow; let him appear, sir.

ARTHUR
You may come near, sir.

FRIPPERY
O welcome, welcome; what's your pawn, sir?

SECOND FELLOW

Faith, a gentlewoman's whole suit, sir.

FRIPPERY
Whole suit? 'Tis well.

SECOND FELLOW
A poor, kind soul, troubled with a bad husband; one that puts her to her shifts here.

FRIPPERY
He puts here from her shifts, methinks, when she is fain to pawn her clothes.

SECOND FELLOW
Look you, sir; a fair satin gown, new taffeta petticoat—

FRIPPERY
Stay, this petticoat has been turned.

SECOND FELLOW
Often turned up and down, and you will, but never turned, sir.

FRIPPERY
Cry you mercy, indeed.

SECOND FELLOW
A fine white beaver, pearl band, three falls; I ha' known her have more in her days.

FRIPPERY
Alas, and she be but a gentlewoman of any count or charge, three falls are nothing in these days! Know that: tut, the world's changed; gentlewomen's falls stand upright now; no sin but has a bolster, that it may lie at ease. Well, what do you borrow of these, sir?

SECOND FELLOW
Twelve pounds, and you will, sir.

FRIPPERY
How?

SECOND FELLOW
They were not her's for twenty.

FRIPPERY
Why, so; our pawn is ever thrice the value of our money, unless in plate and jewels; how should the months be restored and the use else? We must cast it for the twelvemonth, so many pounds, so many months, so many eighteenpences; then the use of these eighteenpences; then the want of the return of those pounds: all these must be laid together; which well considered, the valuation of the pawn had need to sound treble. Can six pound pleasure the gentlewoman?

SECOND FELLOW

It may please her, but, like a man of three-score, in the limberest degree.

FRIPPERY
I have but one word more to say in't; twenty nobles is all and the utmost that I will hazard upon't.

SECOND FELLOW
She must be content with't: the less borrowed, the better paid; come.

FRIPPERY
Arthur.

ARTHUR
At hand, sir.

FRIPPERY
Tell out twenty nobles, and take her name in a bill.

SECOND FELLOW
I'm satisfied, sir.

[Exit with **ARTHUR**.

FRIPPERY
Welcome, good Saint Martin's-in-the-Field, welcome, welcome! I know no other name.

[Enter **PRIMERO**.

PRIMERO
What, so hard at your prayers?

FRIPPERY
A little, sir; summing up my pawns here—what, Master Primero, is it you, sir gallant? And how does all the pretty, sweet ladies, those plump, kind, delicate blisses, ha? whom I kiss in my very thoughts? How do they, gallant?

PRIMERO
Why, gallant, if they should not do well in my house, where should it be done, boy? Have I not a glorious situation?

FRIPPERY
O, a gallant receipt: violet air, curious garden, quaint walks, fantastical arbours, three back doors, and a coach-gate! Nay, thou'rt admirably seated: little furniture will serve thee; thou'rt never without moveables.

PRIMERO
Ay, praise my stars! Ah, the goodly virginities that have been cut up in my house, and the goodly patrimonies that have lain like sops in the gravy! And when those sops were eaten, yet the meat was

kept whole for another, and another, and another; for as in one pie twenty may dip their sippits, so upon one woman forty may consume their patrimonies.

FRIPPERY
Excellent, Master Primero!

PRIMERO
Well, I'll pray for women while I live;
They're the profitablest fools, I'll say that for 'em,
A man can keep about his house; the prettiest kind fowl,
So tame, so gentle, e'en to strangers' hands
So soon familiar, suffer to be touch'd
Of those they ne'er saw twice: the dove's not like 'em.

FRIPPERY
Most certain, for that's honest: but I have
A suit to you.

PRIMERO
And so have I to you.

FRIPPERY
That happens well: grant mine, and I'll grant yours.

PRIMERO
A match.

FRIPPERY
Make me perfect in that trick that got you so much at primero.

PRIMERO
O, for the thread tied at your partner's leg,
The twitch?

FRIPPERY
Ay, that twitch and you call't so.

PRIMERO
That secret twitch got me five hundred pound
Ere 'twas first known, and since I ha' sold it well:
Five hundred pound laid down shall not yet buy
The fee-simple of my twitch: I would be here with't.
'Twas a best invention;
I'd been a beggar many a lousy year
But for my twitch: it was the prettiest twitch!
Many over-cheated gulls have fatted
Me with the bottom of their patrimonies,
E'en to the last sop, gaped while I fed 'em,

Who now live by that art that first undid 'em,
But I must swear you to be secret, close.

FRIPPERY
As a maid at ten.

PRIMERO
Had you sworn but two years higher
I would ne'er ha' believ'd you.

FRIPPERY
Nay, I let twelve alone,
For after twelve has struck, maids look for one.

PRIMERO
I look for one too, and a maid, I think.

FRIPPERY
What, to come hither?

PRIMERO
Sure, she follows me:
A pretty, fat-eyed wench, with a Venus in her cheek; did but raiment smile upon her, she were nectar for great dons, boy: and that's my suit to thee.

FRIPPERY
And that's granted already. Of what volume is this book, that I may fit a cover to't?

PRIMERO
Faith, neither in folio nor in decimo sexto, but in octavo, between both; a pretty, middle-sized trug.

FRIPPERY
Then I have fitted her already, in my eye, i'faith. Here came a pawn in e'en now will make shift to serve her as fit! Look you, sir gallant: satin, taffeta, beaver, fall, and all.

PRIMERO
Is it new?

FRIPPERY
New? You see it bears her youth as freshly.

PRIMERO
A pretty suit of clothes, i'faith: but put case the party should come to redeem 'em of a sudden?

FRIPPERY
Pooh, then your wit's sickly: have not I the policy, think you, to seem extreme busy, and defer 'em till the morrow? Against which time that pawn shall be secretly fetched home, and another carried out to supply the place.

PRIMERO
I like thy craft well there.

FRIPPERY
A general course. O, frippery is an unknown benefit, sir gallant!

PRIMERO
And what must I give you for the hire now, i'faith?

FRIPPERY
Of the whole suit, for the month?

PRIMERO
Ay, for the month.

FRIPPERY
Go to, you shall give me but twelvepence a-day; Master Primero, you're a friend, and I'll use you so: 'tis got up at your house in an afternoon, i'faith, the hire of the whole month. Ye must think I can distinguish spirits, and put a difference between you and others; you pay no more, i'faith.

PRIMERO
I could have offered you no less myself.

FRIPPERY
Tut, a man must use a friend as a friend may use him: your house has been a sweet house to me, both for pleasure and profit; I'll give you your due: omne tulit punctum, you have always kept fine punks in your house, that's for pleasure, qui miscuit utile dulci, and I have had sweet pawns from 'em, that's for profit now.

PRIMERO
You flatter, you flatter, sir gallant. But whist! Here she enters: I prithee, question her.

[Enter **NOVICE**.

O, you're welcome!

FRIPPERY
Is this your new scholar, Master Primero?

PRIMERO
Marry, is she, sir.

FRIPPERY
I'll commend your judgment in a wench while I live: that face will get money, i'faith; 'twill be a get-penny, I warrant you. [To **NOVICE**] Go to, your fortune was choice, pretty bliss, to fall into the regard of so kind a gentleman.

NOVICE
I hope so, sir.

FRIPPERY
See what his care has provided already for you; you'll be simply set out to the world! If you'll have that care now to deserve his pains, O, that will be acceptable! And these be the rudiments you must chiefly point at: to counterfeit cunningly, to wind in gentlemen with powerful attraction to keep his house in name and custom, to dissemble with your own brother, never to betray your fellows' imperfections nor lay open the state of their bodies to strangers, to believe those that give you, to gull those that believe you, to laugh at all under taffeta; and these be your rudiments.

PRIMERO
There's e'en all, i'faith; we'll trouble you with no more. Nay, you shall live at ease enough: for nimming away jewels and favours from gentlemen, which are your chief vails, I hope that will come naturally enough to you, I need not instruct you; you'll have that wit, I trust, to make the most of your pleasure.

NOVICE
I hope one's mother-wit will serve for that, sir.

PRIMERO
O, properest of all, wench! It must be a she-wit that does those things, and thy mother was quick enough at it in her days.

FRIPPERY
Give me leave, sister, to examine you upon two or three particulars: and make you ready, be not ashamed; here's none but friends. Are you a maid?

NOVICE
Yes, in the last quarter, sir.

FRIPPERY
Very proper, that's e'en going out: a maid in the last quarter, that's a whore in the first. Let me see, new moon on Thursday; she'll be changed by that time, too. Are you willing to pleasure gentlemen?

NOVICE
We are all born to pleasure our country, forsooth.

FRIPPERY
Excellent! Can you carry yourself cunningly, and seem often holy?

NOVICE
O, fear not that, sir! My friends were all Puritans.

FRIPPERY
I'll ne'er try her further.

PRIMERO
She's done well, i'faith: I fear not now to turn her loose to any gentleman in Europe.

FRIPPERY
You need not, sir: of her own accord, I think she'll be loose enough without turning. Arthur!

[Enter **ARTHUR**.

ARTHUR
Here, sir.

FRIPPERY
Go, make haste, shift her into that suit presently.

ARTHUR
It shall be done.

PRIMERO
Arthur, do't neatly, Arthur.

ARTHUR
Fear't not, sir.

PRIMERO
Follow him, wench.

NOVICE
With all my heart, sir.

[Exeunt **ARTHUR** and **NOVICE**.

PRIMERO
But, mass, sir,
In what are we forgetful all this while!

FRIPPERY
In what?

PRIMERO
The wooing business, man.

FRIPPERY
Heart, that's true!

PRIMERO
The gallants will prevent us.

FRIPPERY
Are you certain?

PRIMERO
I can avouch it: there's a general meeting
At the deceas'd knight's house this afternoon;
There's rivalship enough.

FRIPPERY
No doubt in that:
Would either thou or I might bear her from 'em!

PRIMERO
My hopes are not yet faint.

FRIPPERY
Nor mine.

PRIMERO
Tut, man.
Nothing in women's hearts sooner wins place
Than a grave outside and an impudent face.

FRIPPERY
And for both those we'll fit it.

PRIMERO
Ay, if the devil
Be not in't: make haste.

FRIPPERY
I follow straight.

[Exit **PRIMERO**.

Vanish, thou fog, and sink beneath our brightness,
Abashed at the splendour of such beams!
We scorn thee, base eclipser of our glories,
That wouldst have hid our shine from mortal's eyes.
Now, gallants, I'm for you, ay, and perhaps before you:
You can appear but glorious from yourselves,
And have your beams but drawn from your own light,
But mine from many: many make me bright.
Here's a diamond that sometimes graced the finger of a countess; here sits a ruby that ne'er lins blushing for the party that pawned it; here a sapphire. O providence and fortune! My beginning was so poor, I would fain forget it; and I take the only course, for I scorn to think on't; slave to a trencher, observer of a salt-cellar, privy to nothing but a closestool, or such unsavoury secrets: but as I strive to forget the days of my serving, so I shall once remember the first step of my rising; for, having hardly raked five mark together, I rejoiced so in that small stock, which most providentially I ventured by water to Blackwall among fishwives; and in small time, what by weekly return and gainful restitution, it rize to a great body, beside a dish of fish for a present, that stately preserved me a seven-night.

Nor ceas'd it there, but drew on greater profit;
For I was held religious by those
That do profess like abstinence,
And was full often secretly supplied
By charitable Catholics,
Who censur'd me sincerely abstinate,
When merely I for hunger, not for zeal,
Eat up the fish, and put their alms to use!
Ha, ha, ha!
But those times are run out; and, for my sake,
Zealous dissemblance has since far'd the worse.
Let me see now, whose cloak shall I wear today to continue change? O Arthur!

[Enter **ARTHUR**.

ARTHUR
Here, sir.

FRIPPERY
Bring down Sir Oliver Needy's taffeta cloak and beaver hat—I am sure he is fast enough in the knight's ward—and Andrew Lucifer's rapier and dagger with the embossed girdle and hangers,

[Exit **ARTHUR**.

—for he's in his third sweat by this time, sipping of the doctor's bottle, or picking the ninth part of a rack of mutton, dry-roasted, with a leash of nightcaps on his head like the pope's triple crown, and as many pillows crushed to his back, with, "O the needles!" For he got the pox of a sempster, and it pricked so much more naturally. Quick, Arthur, quick!

[Enter **ARTHUR** with the pawned items, which **FRIPPERY** puts on.

Now to the deceas'd knight's daughter,
Whom many gallants sue to, I 'mongst many;
For since impudence gains more respect than virtue,
And coin than blood, which few can now deny,
Who're your chief gallants then but such as I?

[Exeunt.

SCENE II - A Room in Katherine's House

Enter **KATHERINE** and **FITSGRAVE**.

FITSGRAVE
You do your beauties injury, sweet virgin,
To lose the time they must rejoice in youth:

There's no perfection in a woman plac'd
But wastes itself though it be never wasted;
Then judge your wrongs yourself.

KATHERINE
Good Master Fitsgrave,
Through sorrow for the knight my father's death,
Whose being was the perfection of my joy
And crown of my desires, I cannot yet
But forcedly on marriage fix my heart:
Yet heaven forbid I should deject your hopes!
Conceive not of me so uncharitably;
I should belie my soul if I should say
You are the man I never should affect.
I understand you thus far, you're a gentleman,
Whom your estate and virtues may command
To a far worthier breast than this of mine.

FITSGRAVE
O cease! I dare not hear such blasphemy.
What is without you worthy I neglect;
In you is plac'd the worth that I respect.
Vouchsafe, unequall'd virgin, to accept
This worthless favour from your servant's arm,
The hallow'd beads, whereon I justly kept
The true and perfect number of my sighs.
Gives a chain of pearl.

KATHERINE
Mine cannot equal yours, yet in exchange
Accept and wear it for my sake.

[Gives a jewel.

FITSGRAVE
Even as my life I'll rate it.

[Enter **GOLDSTONE**, **PURSENET**, **TAILBY**, **FRIPPERY**, **PRIMERO**, and **BOY**, at the farther door.

GOLDSTONE
Heart! Fitsgrave in such bosom single-loves?

PURSENET
So close and private with her!

TAILBY
Observe 'em; he grows proud and bold.

FRIPPERY
Why, was not this a general meeting?

PRIMERO
By her own consent. Death, how I could taste his blood!

KATHERINE
See, the gentlemen,
At my request, do all present themselves.

GOLDSTONE
Manifold blisses wait on her desire,
Whose beauty and whose mind so many honour!

KATHERINE
I take your wishes thankfully, kind gentlemen,
All here assembled, over whose long suits
I ne'er insulted;
Nor, like that common sickness of our sex,
Grew proud in the abundance of my suitors,
Or number of the days they sued unto me.
Dutiful sorrow for my father's death,
Not wilful coyness, hath my hours detain'd
So long in silence.
I'm left to mine own choice: so much the more
My care calls on me. If I err through love,
'Tis I must chide myself; I cannot shift
The fault unto my parents, they're at rest,
And I shall sooner err through love than wealth.

GOLDSTONE
Good!

PURSENET
Excellent!

TAILBY
That likes me well.

PRIMERO
Hope still.

KATHERINE
And my affections do pronounce you all
Worthy their pure and most entire deserts:
Yet they can choose but one;
Nor do I dissuade any of his hopes,
Because my heart is not yet thoroughly fix'd

On marriage or the man,
But crave the quiet respite of one month,
The month unto this night; against which time
I do invite you all to that election,
Which, on my unstain'd faith and virgin promise,
Shall light amongst no strangers, but yourselves.
May this content you?

[While she is speaking, the **BOY** steals from her the chain of pearl.

ALL
Glad and content.

KATHERINE
'Tis a good time to leave;
Till then commend us to your gentlest thoughts.

[Exit.

ALL
Enough.

FITSGRAVE
Ough!

[The **GALLANTS** look scurvily upon **FITSGRAVE**, and he upon them. Exeunt **GOLDSTONE**, **TAILBY**, **FRIPPERY**, and **PRIMERO**. As **PURSENET** is going out, the **BOY** takes him into a corner.

BOY
Hist, master, hist!

PURSENET
Boy, how now?

BOY
Look you, sir.

PURSENET
Her chain of pearl?

BOY
I sneck'd it away finely.

PURSENET
Active boy,
Thy master's best revenue, his life and soul!
Thou keep'st 'em both together: whip away.

[Exit **BOY**.

[Aside] Fall back, fall belly, I must be maintained:
Hope is no purchase;
Nor care I if I miss her. Why I rank
In this design with gallants, there's full cause;
Policy invites me to it:
'Tis not for love, or for her sake alone;
It keeps my state suspectless and unknown.

[Exit.

FITSGRAVE
Their looks run through and through me, and the stings
Of their snake-hissing whispers pierc'd my hearing.
They're mad she grac'd me with one private minute
Above their fortunes: I've observed 'em often
Most spitefully aspected toward my happiness,
Beyond all others; but the cause I know not.
A quiet month the virgin has enclos'd
Unto herself; suitors stand without till then:
In which space cunningly I'll wind myself
Into their bosoms. I've bethought the shape;
Some credulous scholar, easily infected
With fashion, time, and humour: unto such
Their deepest thoughts will, like to wanton fishes,
Play above water, and be all parts seen:
For since at me their envy pines, I'll see
Whether their lives from touch of blame sit free.

[Exit.

ACT II

SCENE I - A Room in Primero's House

Enter **PRIMERO**, meeting **MISTRESS NEWCUT**.

PRIMERO
Mistress Newcut, welcome: here will be choice of gallants for you anon.

MISTRESS NEWCUT
Is all clear? May I venture? Am I not seen of the wicked?

PRIMERO

Strange absurdity, that you should come into my house, and ask if you be not seen of the wicked! Push! I take't unkindly, i'faith: what think you of my house? 'Tis no such common receptacle.

MISTRESS NEWCUT
Forgive me, sweet Master Primero: I can be content to have my pleasure as much as another, but I must have a care of my credit; I would not be seen anything else. My husband's at sea, and a woman shall have an ill report in this world, let her carry herself never so secretly; you know't, Master Primero. And what choice of gallants be they? Will they be proper gentlemen, think you?

PRIMERO
Nay, sure they are as proper as they will be already.

MISTRESS NEWCUT
And I must have choice, you know; I come for no gain, but for sheer pleasure and affection.

PRIMERO
You see your old spy-hole yonder; take your stand, please your own eye. I'll work it so, the gallants shall present themselves before you, and in the most conspicuous fashion.

MISTRESS NEWCUT
That's all I can desire aside till better come.—Look you.

PRIMERO
What mean you, lady?

MISTRESS NEWCUT
A trifle, sir, to buy you silver spurs. Good sir, accept it.

[Gives money and retires.

PRIMERO
Silver spurs? A pretty emblem! Mark it; all her gifts are about riding still: the other day she sent me boot-hose wrought in silk and gold; now silver spurs. Well, go thy ways, thou'rt as profitable a spirit as e'er lighted into my house. Come, ladies, come, 'tis late; to music. When?

[Enter **COURTESANS** and **NOVICE**.

FIRST COURTESAN
You're best command us, sir! Our pimp's grown proud.

PRIMERO
To fools and strangers these are gentlewomen
Of sort and worship, knight's heirs, great in portions,
Boarded here for their music;
And oftentimes 't 'as been so cunningly carried,
That I have had two stolen away at once,
And married at Savoy, and prov'd honest shopkeepers:
And I may safely swear they practis'd music;

They're natural at prick-song. A small mist
Will dazzle a fool's eye, and that's the world:
So I can thump my hand upon the table
With an austere grace, and cry, "One, two, and three,"
Fret, stamp, and curse, foh, 'twill pass well for me.

[Enter **BOY**.

How now, sirrah?

BOY
They're coming in, sir, and strangers in their company.

PRIMERO
Tune apace, ladies. [To **BOY**] Be ready for the song, sirrah.

[Enter **GOLDSTONE, PURSENET, FRIPPERY, TAILBY, FITSGRAVE** disguised, and **BUNGLER**.

GOLDSTONE
Nay, I beseech you, gallants, be more inward with this gentleman; his parts deserve it.

PURSENET
Whence comes he, sir?

GOLDSTONE
Piping hot from the university; he smells of buttered loaves yet; an excellent scholar, [Aside] but the arrantest ass!

[Presenting **BUNGLER**]

For this our solicitor, he's a rare fellow five-and-forty mile hence, believe that: his friends are of the old fashion, all in their graves; and now has he the leisure to follow all new fashions, ply the brothels, practise salutes and cringes.

PURSENET
O!

GOLDSTONE
Now dear acquaintance,
I'll bring you to see fashions.

FITSGRAVE
What house is this, sir?

GOLDSTONE
O, of great name: here music is profess'd;
Here sometimes ladies practise, and the meanest,
Daughters to men of worship,

Whom gentlemen, such as ourselves, may visit,
Court, clip, and exercise our wits upon;
It is a profess'd courtesy.

FITSGRAVE
A pretty recreation, i'faith!

GOLDSTONE
I seldom saw so few here: you shall have 'em sometimes in every corner of the house, with their viols betwixt their legs, and play the sweetest strokes; 'twould e'en filch your soul almost out of your bosom.

FITSGRAVE
Pax on't, we spoil ourselves for want of these things at university.

GOLDSTONE
You have no such natural happiness: let's draw near.

PRIMERO
Gentlemen, you are all most respectively welcome.

GOLDSTONE
We are bold and insatiate suitors, sir, to the breath of your music, and the dear sight of those ladies.

PRIMERO
And what our poor skill can invite you to,
You're kindly welcome: you must pardon 'em, gentlemen,
Virgins and bashful, besides new beginners:
'Tis not a whole month since they were first enter'd.

GOLDSTONE [Aside]
Seven year in my knowledge.

PRIMERO
They blush at their very lessons; they'll not endure
To hear of a stop, a prick, or a semiquaver.

FIRST COURTESAN
O, out upon you!

PRIMERO
La, I tell you. You'll bear me witness, gentlemen,
If their complaints come to their parents' ears,
They're words of art I teach 'em, nought but art.

GOLDSTONE
Why, 'tis most certain.

BUNGLER

For all scholars know that musica est ars.

ALL THE COURTESANS
O, beastly word!

PRIMERO
Look to the ladies, gentlemen.

GOLDSTONE
Kiss again.

PURSENET
Come, another.

TAILBY
This a good interim.

[Exit.

PRIMERO
What have you done, sir?

BUNGLER
Why, what have I done?

PRIMERO
Saw you their stomachs queasy, and come with such gross meat?

BUNGLER
Why, is't not Latin, sir?

PRIMERO
Latin? Why, then, let the next to't be Latin too.

PURSENET
So, enough.

GOLDSTONE
Nay, I can assure you thus far, I that never knew the language have heard so much that ars is Latin for art; and it may well be, too, for there's more art in't nowadays than ever was.

PRIMERO
Is't possible?
I'm sorry then I've followed it so far.

FIRST COURTESAN
A scholar call you him?

PRIMERO
Music must not jar:
The offence is satisfied. Come, to the song;
Begin, sir.

[*The song; and he keeps time, shows several humours and moods: the* **BOY** *in his pocket nims away Fitsgrave's jewel here, and exit.*]

BUNGLER
Not a whole month since you were entered, ladies?

FITSGRAVE [Aside]
None that shall see their cunning will believe it.

PRIMERO
It is no affliction, gentlemen.

BUNGLER
I care not much, i'faith, if I write down to my father presently to send up my sister in all haste that I may place her here at this music-school.

MISTRESS NEWCUT [Looking in]
'Slid, 'tis the fool my cousin! I would not for the value of three recreations he had seen me here.

PRIMERO
How like you your new prize?

BUNGLER
Pray, give me leave;
I have not yet sufficiently admir'd her.

PRIMERO
My wits must not stand idle. 'Slife, he's in a sick trance!

GOLDSTONE [Aside]
A cheat or two among these mistresses
Would not be ill bestow'd; I affect none,
But for my prey: such are their affections,
I know it; how could drabs and cheaters live else?
Then since the world rolls on dissimulation,
I'll be the first dissembler.

FIRST COURTESAN
Prithee, love, comfort, choice,
My only wish, in thee I am confin'd!
Deny me anything, a slight chain of pearl?

PURSENET

Nay, an't be but slight—

FIRST COURTESAN
Being denied,
I prize it slight; but given me by my love,
Light shall not be so dear unto my eye,
Mine eye unto the body, as the gift.

PURSENET
How have I power to deny this to you,
That command all? My fortunes are thy servants,
And thou the mistress both of them and me.

[Gives her the chain.

FIRST COURTESAN
The truest that e'er breathed!

GOLDSTONE
To a gentleman
That thus so long has so sincerely lov'd you
As I myself, ne'er was less pity shown.

SECOND COURTESAN
Why, I never was held cruel.

GOLDSTONE
But to me.

SECOND COURTESAN
Nor to you.

GOLDSTONE
Go to, 't 'as scar'd you much.

SECOND COURTESAN
I'm sorry your conceit is so unkind
To think me so.

GOLDSTONE
When had I other argument?
I've often tender'd you my love and service,
And that in no mean fashion;
Yet were you ne'er that requiteful mistress
That grac'd me with one favour;
'Slight, not so much as such a pretty ring;
Pax on't, 't'as almost broke my heart.

[Takes off her ring.

SECOND COURTESAN
Has took it off! 'Sfoot, Master Goldstone!

GOLDSTONE
Nay, where a man loves most, there to be scanted!

SECOND COURTESAN
My ring, come, come—

GOLDSTONE
What reckon I a satin gown or two,
If she were wise?

SECOND COURTESAN
Life! My ring, sir, come—

GOLDSTONE
Have you the face, i'faith?

SECOND COURTESAN
Give me my ring.

GOLDSTONE
Prithee, hence; by this light you get none on't.

SECOND COURTESAN
How?

GOLDSTONE
I hold your favours of more pure esteem,
Than to part from 'em; faith, I do, howe'er
You think of me.

SECOND COURTESAN
Push, pray, sir—

GOLDSTONE
Hark you, go to;
You've lost much by unkindness; go your ways.

SECOND COURTESAN
'Sfoot!

GOLDSTONE
But yet there's no time past; you may redeem it.

SECOND COURTESAN
Come, I cannot miss it, i' faith; beside,
The gentleman that bestowed it on me
Swore to me it cost him twenty nobles.

GOLDSTONE
Twenty nobles? Pox of twenty nobles!
But you must cost me more, you pretty villain:
Ah, you little rogue!

SECOND COURTESAN
Come, come, I know you're but in jest.

GOLDSTONE
In jest? No, you shall see.

SECOND COURTESAN
No way will get it:
[Aside] As good give it him now, and hope for somewhat.

GOLDSTONE
True love made jest!

SECOND COURTESAN
I did but try thy faith,
How fast thou'dst hold it. Now I see a woman
May venture worthy favours to thy trust,
And have 'em truly kept; and I protest,
Had I drawn't from thee, I should ne'er ha' lov'd thee;
I know that.

GOLDSTONE
'Sfoot, I was ne'er so wronged in my life!
Think you I'm in jest with you? What, with my love?
I could find lighter subjects, you shall see;
And time will show how much you injure me.

SECOND COURTESAN
The ring, were it thrice worth, I freely give,
For I know you'll requite it.

GOLDSTONE
Will I live?

SECOND COURTESAN
Enough.

GOLDSTONE [Aside]

Why, this was well come off now:
Where's my old serving-man? Not yet return'd?
O, here he peeps.

[Enter **FULK**.

Now, sirrah?

FULK
May it please your worship: they're done artificially, i'faith, boy.

GOLDSTONE
Both the great beakers?

FULK
Both, lad.

GOLDSTONE
Just the same size?

FULK
Ay, and the marks as just.

GOLDSTONE
So, fall off respectively now.

FULK
My lord desires your worship of all love—

GOLDSTONE
His lordship must hold me excused till morning; I'll not break company tonight. Where sup we, gallants?

PURSENET
At Mermaid.

GOLDSTONE
Sup there who list, I have forsworn the house.

FULK [Aside]
For the truth is, this plot must take effect at Mitre.

[Exit.

PURSENET
Faith, I'm indifferent.

BUNGLER
So are we, gentlemen.

PURSENET
Name the place, Master Goldstone.

GOLDSTONE
Why, the Mitre, in my mind, for neat attendance, diligent boys, and, push, excels it far!

ALL
Agreed, the Mitre then.

PURSENET
Boy! [Aside] Some goodness toward: the boy's whipped away.

FITSGRAVE
The jewel, heart, the jewel!

GOLDSTONE
How now, sir? What mov'd you?

FITSGRAVE
Nothing, sir;
A spice of poetry, a kind a' fury,
A disease runs among scholars.

GOLDSTONE
Mass, it made you stamp.

FITSGRAVE
Whew,
'Twill make some stamp and stare, make a strange noise,
Curse, swear, beat tire-men, and kick players' boys;
The effects are very fearful.

PURSENET
Bless me from't!

FITSGRAVE
O, you need not fear it, sir. [Aside] Hell of this luck!

GOLDSTONE
Hark, he's at it again!

PURSENET
Some pageant-plot,
Or some device for the tilt-yard: disturb him not.

FITSGRAVE [Aside]
How can I gain her love, when I have lost her favour?

GOLDSTONE
What money hast about thee? Look you, sir, I must be fain to pawn a fair stone here for ordinary expenses: a pox of my tenants! I give 'em twenty days after the quarter, and they cut out forty.

FRIPPERY
Why, you might take the forfeiture of their leases then.

GOLDSTONE
I know I might; but what's their course? The rogues come me up all together, with geese and capons, and petitions in pigs' snouts, which would move any man, i'faith, were his stomach ne'er so great; and to see how pitifully the pullen will look, it makes me after relent, and turn my anger into a quick fire to roast 'em—nay, touch't and spare it not.

FRIPPERY
'Tis right: well, what does your worship borrow of this, sir?

GOLDSTONE
The stone's twenty nobles.

FRIPPERY
Nay, hardly.

GOLDSTONE
As I am a right gentleman.

FRIPPERY
It comes near it indeed: well, here's five pound in gold upon't.

GOLDSTONE
'Twill serve; and the ring safe and secret?

FRIPPERY
As a virgin's.

GOLDSTONE
I wish no higher. What, gallants, are you constant? Does the place hold?

ALL
The Mitre.

GOLDSTONE
Sir, in regard of our continued boldness and trouble, which love to your music hath made us guilty of, shall we entreat your worship's company, with these sweet ladies, your professed scholars, to take part of a poor supper with myself and these gentlemen at the Mitre?

FRIPPERY
Pray, Master Primero.

PURSENET
I beseech you, sir, let it be so.

PRIMERO
O, pardon me, sweet gentlemen; the world's apt to censure. I have the charge of them, they're left in trust, they're virgins: and I dare not hazard their fames; the least touch mars 'em: and what would their right worshipful parents think, if the report should fly to them, that they were seen with gentlemen in a tavern?

GOLDSTONE
All this may be prevented: what serves your coach for?
They may come coach'd and mask'd.

PRIMERO
You put me to't, sir;
Yet I must say again, I fear the drawers
And vintner's boys will be familiar with them,
And think 'em mistresses.

PURSENET
There are those places where respect seems slighter;
More censure is belonging to the Mitre?
You know that, sir.

PRIMERO
Gentlemen, you prevail.

GOLDSTONE
We'll all expect you there.

PRIMERO
And we'll not fail.

FITSGRAVE
The devil will ne'er dissemble with them so,
As you for them.

GOLDSTONE
Come, sir.

FRIPPERY
What else? Let's go.

[Exeunt all except **PRIMERO**, **COURTESANS** and **NOVICE**. Enter **TAILBY**.

PRIMERO
How cheer you, sir?

TAILBY
Faith, like the moon, more bright,
Decreas'd in body, but re-made in light;
Here thou shalt share some of my brightness with me.

[Gives **PRIMERO** gold.

PRIMERO
By my faith, they're comfortable beams, sir.

FIRST COURTESAN
Come,
Where have you spent the time now from my sight?
I'm jealous of thy action.

TAILBY
Push! I did but walk
A turn or two in the garden.

FIRST COURTESAN
What made you there?

TAILBY
Nothing but cropp'd a flower.

FIRST COURTESAN
Some woman's honour, I believe.

TAILBY [Showing her a flower]
Foh! Is this a woman's honour?

FIRST COURTESAN
Much about one,
When both are pluck'd, their sweetness is soon gone.

TAILBY
Prithee, be true to me.

FIRST COURTESAN
When did I fail?

TAILBY
Yet I am ever doubtful that you sin.

FIRST COURTESAN
I do account the world but as my spoil,
To adorn thee:

My love is artificial to all others,
But purity to thee. Dost thou want gold?
Here, take this chain of pearl, supply thyself:
Be thou but constant, firm, and just to me,
Rich heirs shall want ere want come near to thee.

TAILBY
Upon thy lip I seal sincerity.

[Exit **FIRST COURTESAN**.

SECOND COURTESAN
Was this your vow to me?

TAILBY
Pox, what's a kiss to be quite rid of her?
She's su'd so long, I was asham'd of her:
'Twas but her cheek I kiss'd neither, to save her longing.

SECOND COURTESAN
'Tis not a kiss I weigh.

TAILBY
Had you weigh'd this,
'T 'ad lack'd above five ounces of a true one;
No kiss that e'er weigh'd lighter.

SECOND COURTESAN
'Tis thy love that I suspect.

TAILBY
My love? Why, by this— What shall I swear by?

SECOND COURTESAN
Swear by this jewel; keep thy oath, keep that.

TAILBY
By this jewel, then, no creature can be perfect
In my love but thy dear self.

SECOND COURTESAN
I rest content.

[Exit.

TAILBY
Ha, ha, ha! Let's laugh at 'em, sweet soul.

NOVICE
Ay, they may laugh at me;
I was a novice, and believ'd your oaths.

TAILBY
Why, what do you think of me? Make I no difference
'Tween seven years' prostitution and seven days?
Why, you're but in the wane of a maid yet.
You wrong my health in thinking I love them:
Do not I know their populous imperfections?
Why, they cannot live till Easter,
Let 'em show the fairest side to th' world,
Like hundreds more, whose clothes e'en stand upright
In silver, when their bodies are ready
To drop through 'em; such there be; they may deceive
The world, they ne'er shall me.

NOVICE
Forgive my doubts;
And for some satisfaction wear this ring,
From which I vow'd ne'er but to thee to part.

TAILBY
With which thou ever bind'st me to thy heart.

[Exeunt.

SCENE II - A street

Enter **FITSGRAVE**.

FITSGRAVE
My pocket pick'd? This was no brothel-house!
A music school? Damnation has fine shapes:
I paid enough for the song, I've lost a jewel
To me more precious than their souls to them
That gave consent to filch it. I'll hunt hard,
Waste time and money, trace and wheel about,
But I will find these secret mischiefs out.

[Enter **SERVANT**.

[Aside] How now? What's he?
O, a servant to my love: being thus disguis'd,
I'll learn some news.—Now, sir? You belong to me.

SERVANT
I do, sir; but I cannot stay to say so. Nay, good sir, detain me not; I am going in all haste to inquire or lay wait for a chain of pearl, nimmed out of her pocket the fifth of November, a dismal day.

FITSGRAVE
Ha! A chain of pearl, sayst thou?

SERVANT
A chain of pearl, sir, which one Master Fitsgrave, a gentleman and a suitor, fastened upon her as a pledge of his love.

FITSGRAVE
Ha!

SERVANT
Urge me no more, I have no more to say
Your friend, Jeronimo Bedlam.

[Exit.

FITSGRAVE
Thou'rt a mad fellow indeed.
Some comfort yet, that hers is missing too;
I feel my soul at much more ease: both stol'n!
When griefs have partners they are better borne.

[Exit.

SCENE III - A Room in Primero's House

Enter **TAILBY**.

TAILBY [Singing]
O, the parting of us twain
Hath caus'd me mickle pain!
And I shall ne'er be married
Until I see my muggle again.

MISTRESS NEWCUT [Looking in]
Hist!

PRIMERO
Ha?

MISTRESS NEWCUT
The nimble gentleman, in the celestial stockings—

PRIMERO
Has the best smock-fortune to be beloved of women. [Singing] Valle loo lo, lille lo lillo, valle loo lee lo lillo!

TAILBY [Singing]
Valle loo lo, lille lo lillo, valle loo lee lo lillo!

MISTRESS NEWCUT
Ah, sweet gentleman, he keeps it up stately!

PRIMERO
Well held, i'faith, sir: mass, and now I remember too, I think you ne'er saw my little banqueting box above since I altered it.

TAILBY
Why, have you altered that?

PRIMERO
O, divinely, sir! The pictures are all new run over again.

TAILBY
Fie!

PRIMERO
For what had the painter done, think you? Drew me Venus naked, which is the grace of a man's room, you know; and, when he had done, drew a number of oaken leaves before her: had not lawn been a hundred times softer, made a better show, and been more gentlewoman-like?

TAILBY
More lady-like a great deal.

PRIMERO
Come, you shall see how 'tis altered now; I do not think but you'll like her.

[Exeunt.

SCENE IV - A Room in the Mitre

Enter all at once: **PRIMERO, COURTESANS, NOVICE, GOLDSTONE, PURSENET, FRIPPERY, TAILBY, BUNGLER, FULK, ARTHUR BOY, BOY,** and **SERVANT.**

PRIMERO
Where be your liveries?

FIRST COURTESAN

They attend without.

PRIMERO
Go, call the coach.

[Exit **SERVANT**.

Gentlemen, you have excelled in kindness as we in boldness.

TAILBY
So you think amiss, sir.

GOLDSTONE
Kind ladies, we commit you to sweet dreams,
Ourselves unto the fortune of the dice.
Dice, ho!

[Exit **PRIMERO**.

FIRST COURTESAN
You rest firm mine?

TAILBY
E'en all my soul to thee.

[Exit **FIRST COURTESAN**.

SECOND COURTESAN
You keep your vows?

TAILBY
Why, do I breathe or see?

[Exit **SECOND COURTESAN**.

NOVICE
Is your love constant?

TAILBY
Ay, to none but thee.

[Exit **NOVICE**.

Now gone, ay, now I love nor them nor thee;
'Slife, I should be cloy'd, should I love one in three.

[Enter **FITSGRAVE**.

PURSENET
O, here's Master Bouser now.

FITSGRAVE
Save you, sweet gentlemen.

TAILBY
Sweet Master Bouser, welcome.

PURSENET
When come these dice?

VINTNER [Within]
Anon, anon, sir.

PURSENET
Yet anon, anon, sir!

GOLDSTONE [Taking **FULK** aside]
Hast thou shown art in 'em?

FULK
You shall be judge, sir; here be the tavernbeakers, and here peep out the fine alchemy knaves, looking like, well, sir, most of our gallants, that seem what they are not.

GOLDSTONE
Peace, villain, am not I in presence?

FULK
Why, that puts me in mind of the jest, sir.

GOLDSTONE
Again, you chatterer?

FULK
Nay, compare 'em, and spare 'em not.

GOLDSTONE
The bigness of the bore, just the same size; the marks, no difference. Away, put money in thy pocket, and offer to draw in upon the least occasion.

FULK
I am no babe, sir.

GOLDSTONE
Hist!

FULK

What's the matter now?

GOLDSTONE
Give me a pair of false dice ere you go.

FULK
Pax on't, you're so troublesome too, you cannot remember a thing before! If I stay a little longer, I shall be staid anon.

[Enter **VINTNER**.

VINTNER
Here be dice for your worships.

PURSENET
Oh, come, come!

GOLDSTONE [Aside]
The vintner himself?
I'll shift away these beakers by a slight.

VINTNER
Master Goldstone—

GOLDSTONE
How now, you conjuring rascal?

VINTNER
Bless your good worship; you're in humours, methinks.

GOLDSTONE
Humours? Say that again.

VINTNER
I said no such word, sir.
[Aside] Would I had my beakers out on's fingers!

GOLDSTONE
What's thy name, vintner?

VINTNER
Jack, and please your worship.

GOLDSTONE
Turn knight, like thy companions, scoundrel, live upon usury, wear thy gilt spurs at thy girdle for fear of slubbering.

VINTNER

Oh no, I hope I shall have more grace than so, sir! Pray, let me help your worship.

GOLDSTONE
Cannot I push 'em together without your help?

VINTNER
O, I beseech your worship! They're the two standards of my house.

GOLDSTONE
Standards? There lie your standards.

VINTNER
Good your worship. [Aside] I am glad they are out of his fingers: my wife shall lock 'em up presently; they shall see no sun this twelvemonth's day for this trick.

GOLDSTONE
Let me come to the sight of your standards again.

VINTNER
Your worship shall pardon me. [Aside] Now you shall not see 'em in haste, I warrant ye.

GOLDSTONE
I do not desire't. Ha, ha!

[Exit **VINTNER** with beakers.

FITSGRAVE
Why, Master Goldstone!

GOLDSTONE
I am for you, gallants. Master Bouser, cry you mercy, sir: why supped you from us?

FITSGRAVE
Faith, sir, I met with a couple of my fellow pupils at university, and so we renewed our acquaintance and supped together.

GOLDSTONE
Fie, that's none of the newest fashion, I must tell you that, Master Bouser: you must never take acquaintance of any 'a th' university when you are at London; nor any of London when you're at university. You must be more forgetful, i'faith; every place ministers his acquaintance abundantly.

BUNGLER
He tells you true, sir.

GOLDSTONE
I warrant you here's a gentleman will ne'er commit such an absurdity.

BUNGLER

Who, I? No: 'tis well known, if I be disposed, I'll forget any man in a seven-night, and yet look him in the face: nay, let him ride but ten mile from me, and come home again, it shall be at my choice whether I'll remember him or no: I have tried that.

GOLDSTONE
This is strange, sir.

BUNGLER
'Tis as a man gives his mind to't, sir: and now you bring me in, I remember 'twas once my fortune to be cozened of all my clothes, and with my clothes my money; a poor shepherd, pitying, me, took me in and relieved me.

GOLDSTONE
'Twas kindly done of him, i'faith.

BUNGLER
Nay, you shall see now: 'twas his fortune likewise, not long after, to come to me in much distress, i'faith, and with weeping eyes; and do you think I remembered him?

GOLDSTONE
You could not choose.

BUNGLER
By my troth, not I; I forgot him quite, and never remembered him to this hour.

GOLDSTONE
And yet knew who he was?

BUNGLER
As well as I know you, i'faith: 'tis a gift given to some above others.

FITSGRAVE [Aside]
To fools and knaves; they never miss on't.

BUNGLER
Does any make such a wonder at this? Why, alas! 'Tis nothing to forget others! What say you to those that forget themselves?

GOLDSTONE
Nay, then, to dice.
Come, set me, gallants, set.

FRIPPERY
Ay, fall to't, gentlemen.
[Aside] I shall hear some news from some of you anon:
I've th' art to know which lose, and ne'er look on.
I'll be ready with all the worst money I can find about me.—
Arthur!

ARTHUR
Here, sir.

FRIPPERY
Stand ready.

ARTHUR
Fear not me, sir.

GOLDSTONE
These are mine, sir.

FRIPPERY [Aside]
Here's a washed angel;
It shall away : here's Mistress Rose-noble
Has lost her maidenhead, crack'd in the ring;
She's good enough for gamesters, and to pass
From man to man: for gold presents at dice
Your harlot, in one hour won and lost thrice;
Every man has a fling at her.

TAILBY
Again? Pax of these dice!

BUNGLER
'Tis ill to curse the dead, sir.

TAILBY
Mew, where should I wish
The pox but among bones?

FITSGRAVE
He tells you right, sir.

TAILBY
I ne'er have any luck at these odd hands;
None here to make us six? Why, Master Frip!

FRIPPERY
I am very well here, I thank you, sir: I had rather be telling my money myself than have others count it for me; 'tis the scurviest music in the world, methinks, to hear my money gingle in other men's pockets; I never had any mind to't, i'faith.

TAILBY
'Slud, play six or play four, I'll play no more.

GOLDSTONE

'Sfoot, you see there's none here to draw in.

FULK
Rather than you should be destitute, gentlemen, I'll play my ten pound, if my master's worship will give me leave.

PURSENET
Come.

TAILBY
He shall, he shall.

GOLDSTONE
Pray, excuse me, gentlemen. [To **FULK**] 'Sfoot, how now, goodman rascal? What, because you served my grandfather when he went ambassador, and got some ten pound by th' hand, has that put such spirit in you to offer to draw in among gentlemen of worship, knave?

TAILBY
Pray, sir, let's entreat so much for once.

PURSENET
'Tis a usual grace, i'faith, sir; you've many gentlemen will play with their men.

BUNGLER
Ay, and with their maids too, i'faith.

PURSENET
Good sir, give him leave.

GOLDSTONE
Yes, come, and you be weary on't; I pray draw near, sir.

FULK
Not so, sir.

TAILBY
Come, fool, fear nothing; I warrant 't ye has given thee leave: stand here by me. Come now, set round, gentlemen, set.

PURSENET
How the poor fellow shakes! Throw lustily, man.

FULK
At all, gentlemen!

TAILBY
Well said, i'faith.

[**FULK** throws the dice.

PURSENET
They're all thine.

TAILBY
By my troth, I am glad the fellow has such luck, 'twill encourage him well.

FULK
At my master's worship alone!

GOLDSTONE
Now, sir slave?

FULK
At my master's worship alone!

GOLDSTONE
So, saucy rascal!

FULK
At my master's worship alone!

GOLDSTONE
You're a rogue, and will be ever one.

FULK
By my troth, gentlemen, at all again for once.

[**FULK** throws the dice.

TAILBY
Take 'em to thee, boy, take 'em to thee; thou'rt worthy of 'em, i'faith.

GOLDSTONE
Gentlemen, faith, I am angry with you: go and suborn my knave again me here, to make him proud and peremptory!

TAILBY
Troth, that's but your conceit, sir; the fellow's an honest fellow, and knows his duty, I dare swear for him.

PURSENET
Heart, I am sick already!

GOLDSTONE
Whither goes Master Pursenet?

PURSENET
Play on; I'll take my turn, sir. Boy!

BOY
Master?

PURSENET
Pist! [Taking him aside] A supply; carry't closely, my little fooker. How much?

BOY
Three pound, sir.

PURSENET
Good boy! Take out another lesson.—How now, gentlemen?

TAILBY
Devil's in't, did you e'er see such a hand?

PURSENET
I set you these three angels.

BOY [Aside]
My master may set high, for all his stakes are drawn out of other men's pockets.

[Exit.

FULK
As I said, gentlemen.

PURSENET
Deuce ace!

FULK
At all your right worshipful worships!

ALL
Death and vengeance!

GOLDSTONE
Hell, darkness!

TAILBY
Hold, sir.

PURSENET
Master Goldstone—

GOLDSTONE

Hinder me not, sweet gentlemen. [To **FULK**] You rascal, I banish thee the board.

TAILBY
I'faith, but you shall not, sir.

GOLDSTONE
Touch a die, and thou darest! Come you in with your lousy ten pound, you slave, among gentlemen of worship, and win thirty at a hand?

TAILBY
Why, will you kick again luck, sir?

BUNGLER
As long as the poor fellow ventures the loss of his own money, who can be offended at his fortunes?

FULK
I have a master here! Many a gentleman would be glad to see his man come forward, aha.

PURSENET
Pray, be persuaded, sir.

GOLDSTONE
'Slife, here's none cuts my throat in play but he; I have observ'd it, an unlucky slave 'tis.

BUNGLER
Methinks his luck's good enough, sir.

GOLDSTONE
Upon condition, gentlemen, that I may ever bar him from the board hereafter, I am content to wink at him.

PURSENET
Faith, use your own pleasure hereafter; h'as won our money now. [To **FULK**] Come to th' table, sir; your master's friends with you.

FULK
Pray, gentlemen—

TAILBY
The fiend's in't, I think: I left a fair chain of pearl at my lodging, too, like an ass, and ne'er remembered it; that would ha' been a good pawn now. [To **FRIPPERY**] Speak, what do you lend upon these, Master Frip?

[Offering his weapons, with girdle and hangers]

I care not much if you take my beaver hat too, for I perceive 'tis dark enough already, and it does but trouble me here.

FRIPPERY

Very well, sir; why, now I can lend you three pound, sir.

TAILBY
Prithee, do't quickly then.

FRIPPERY
There 'tis in six angels.

TAILBY
Very compendiously.

FRIPPERY
Here, Arthur, run away with these presently; I'll enter 'em into th' shopbook tomorrow.

[Exit **ARTHUR** with pawned items.

[Writing] "Item, one gilt hatch'd rapier and dagger, with a fair embroidered girdle and hangers, with which came also a beaver hat with a correspondent band."

TAILBY
Push! I'faith, sir, you're to blame; you have snibbed the poor fellow too much; he can scarce speak, he cleaves his words with sobbing.

FULK
Haff, haff, haff, haff at all, gentlemen.

GOLDSTONE
Ah, rogue, I'll make you know yourself!

FULK
At the fairest!

PURSENET
Out, i'faith! Two aces.

GOLDSTONE
I am glad of that; come, pay me all these, goodman cloak-bag.

PURSENET
Why, are you the fairest, sir?

GOLDSTONE
You need not doubt of that, sir.—Five angels, you scoundrel!

TAILBY
Fie a' these dice! Not one hand tonight! There they go, gentlemen, at all, i'faith!

PURSENET

Pay all with two treys and a quater.

TAILBY
All curses follow 'em! Pay yourselves withal. I'll pawn myself to't, but I'll see a hand tonight: not once hold in! Here, Master Frip, lend me you hand, quick, quick; so.

[Takes off his doublet.]

FRIPPERY
What do you borrow of this doublet now?

TAILBY
Ne'er saw the world three days.

FRIPPERY
Go to; in regard you're a continual customer I'll use you well, and pleasure you with five angels upon't.

TAILBY
Let me not stand too long i' th' cold for them.

BUNGLER
Had ever country gentleman such fortune? All swoopt away! I'd need repair to th' broker's.

TAILBY
If you be in that mind, sir, there sits a gentleman will furnish you upon any pawn as well as the publickst broker of 'em all.

BUNGLER
Say you so, sir? There's comfort in that, i'faith.

FRIPPERY [Writing]
"Item, upon his orange-tawny satin doublet, five angels."

BUNGLER
But, by your leave, sir, next comes the breeches.

FRIPPERY
O, I have tongue fit for anything.

BUNGLER
Saving your tale, sir; 'tis given me to understand that you are a gentleman i' th' hundred, and deal in the premises aforesaid.

FRIPPERY
Master Bungler, Master Bungler, you're mightily mistook: I am content to do a gentleman a pleasure for once, so his pawn be neat and sufficient.

BUNGLER

Why, what say you to my grandfather's seal-ring here?

FRIPPERY
Ay, marry, sir, this is somewhat like.

BUNGLER
Nay, view it well; an ancient arms, I can tell you.

FRIPPERY
What's this, sir?

BUNGLER
The great cod-piece, with nothing in't.

FRIPPERY
How!

BUNGLER
The word about it, Parturiunt montes.

FRIPPERY
What's that, I pray, sir?

BUNGLER
"You promise to mount us."

FRIPPERY
And belike he was not so good as his word?

BUNGLER
So it should seem by the story, for so our names came to be Bunglers.

FRIPPERY
A lamentable hearing, that so great a house should shrink and fall to ruin!

PURSENET
Two quaters, and yet lose it? Heart! Boy!

[Enter **BOY**.

[Aside to him] I'faith, what is't?

BOY [Aside to him]
Five pound, sir.

PURSENET [Aside]
By my troth, this boy goes forward well; ye shall see him come to his preferment i' th' end!

GOLDSTONE
Why, how now? Who's that, gentlemen? A bargeman?

TAILBY
I never have any luck, gallants, till my doublet's off; I'm not half nimble enough at this, old cinque-quater drivel-beard.

FULK
Your worship must pay me all these, sir.

TAILBY
There, and feast the devil with 'em!

PURSENET
Hell gnaw these dice!

GOLDSTONE
What, do you give over, gallants?

FULK [Aside to **GOLDSTONE**]
Is't not time?

TAILBY
I protest I have but one angel left to guide me home to my lodging.

GOLDSTONE [Aside to **FULK**]
How much, thinkest?

FULK [Aside to **GOLDSTONE**]
Some fourscore angels, sir.

GOLDSTONE [Aside to **FULK**]
Peace, we'll join powers anon, and see how strong we are in the whole number. Mass, yon gilt goblet stands so full in mine eye, the whoreson tempts me; it comes like cheese after a great feast, to disgest the rest: he will hardly 'scape me, i'faith, I see that by him already: back for a parting blow now.—Boy!

[Enter **VINTNER**.

VINTNER
Anon, anon, sir.

GOLDSTONE
Fetch a pennyworth of soft wax to seal letters.

VINTNER
I will, sir.

[Exit.

TAILBY
Nay, had not I strange casting? Thrice together two quaters and a deuce!

PURSENET
Why, was not I as often haunted with two treys and a quater?

[Enter **VINTNER**.

VINTNER
There's wax for your worship. [To offstage] Anon, anon, sir.

[Exit.

GOLDSTONE [Aside to **FULK**]
Screen me a little, you whoreson old cross-biter.

FULK [Aside to **GOLDSTONE**]
Why, what's the business? Filch it on hob goblet?

PURSENET
And what has Master Bouser lost?

FITSGRAVE
Faith, not very deeply, sir; enough for a scholar, some half a score royals.

PURSENET
'Sfoot, I have lost as many with spurs at their heels.

[Enter **VINTNER** with two **DRAWERS**.

GOLDSTONE
Come, gallants, shall we stumble?

TAILBY
What's a' clock?

FIRST DRAWER
Here's none on't, Dick; the goblet's carried down.

GOLDSTONE
Nay, 'tis upon the point of three, boy.

SECOND DRAWER
What's to be done, sirs?

VINTNER

All's paid, and your worships are welcome; only there's a goblet missing, gentlemen, and cannot be found about house.

GOLDSTONE
How, a goblet?

PURSENET
What manner a' one?

VINTNER
A gilt goblet, sir, of an indifferent size.

GOLDSTONE
'Sfoot, I saw such a one lately.

VINTNER
It cannot be found now, sir.

GOLDSTONE
Came there no strangers here?

VINTNER
No, sir.

GOLDSTONE
'Tis a marvellous matter, that a goblet should be gone, and none but we in the room; the loss is near all, here as we are; keep the door, vintner.

VINTNER
No, I beseech your worship.

GOLDSTONE
By my troth, vintner, we'll have a privy search for this. What, we are not all one woman's children.

VINTNER
I beseech ye, gentlemen, have not that conceit of me, that I suspect your worships.

GOLDSTONE
Tut, you are an ass; do you know every man's nature? There's a broker i' th' company.

PURSENET [Aside to **BOY**]
'Slife, you have not stole the goblet, boy, have you?

BOY [Aside to **PURSENET**]
Not I, sir.

PURSENET [Aside to **BOY**]
I was afraid.—'Tis a good cause, i'faith, let each man search his fellow: we'll begin with you.

TAILBY
I shall save somebody a labour, gentlemen, for I'm half searched already.

PURSENET
I thought the goblet had hung here, i'faith; none here, nor here.

GOLDSTONE
Seek about floor. What was the goblet worth, vintner?

VINTNER
Three pound ten shillings, sir; no more.

GOLDSTONE
Pox on't, gentlemen, 'tis but angels apiece: it shall be a brace of mine, rather than I would have our reputations breathed upon by all comers; for you must think they'll talk on't in all companies—such a night, in such a company, such a goblet: 'sfoot, it may grow to a gangrene in our credits, and be incurable.

TAILBY
Faith, I am content.

FRIPPERY
So am I.

PURSENET
There's my angel too.

GOLDSTONE
So, and mine. [To **VINTNER**] I'll tell thee what, the missing of this goblet has dismayed the gentlemen much.

VINTNER
I am sorry for that, sir.

GOLDSTONE
Yet they send thee this comfort by me; if they see thee but rest satisfied, and depart away contented, which will appear in thy countenance, not three times thrice the worth of the goblet shall hang between them and thee, both in their continual custom and all their acquaintances.

VINTNER
I thank their worships all; I am satisfied.

GOLDSTONE
Say it again.—Do you hear, gentlemen?

VINTNER
I thank your worships all; I am satisfied.

[Exeunt **VINTNER** and **DRAWERS**.

GOLDSTONE
Why, la, was not this better than hazarding our reputations upon trifles, and in such public as a tavern, such a questionable place?

TAILBY
True.

PURSENET
Faith, it was well thought on.

GOLDSTONE
Nay, keep your way, gentlemen: I have sworn, Master Bouser, I will be last, i'faith.

[Exeunt all except **GOLDSTONE** and **FULK**.

Rascal, the goblet!

FULK
Where, sir?

GOLDSTONE
Peep yon, sir, under.

FULK
Here, sir.

[He draws out the goblet. Exeunt.

ACT III

SCENE I - A Room in Tailby's Lodging

Enter **TAILBY** reading a letter.

TAILBY [Reading]
"My husband is rode from home: make no delay; I know, if your will be as free as your horse, you will see me yet ere dinner. From Kingston, this eleventh of November." Hah! These women are such creatures, such importunate, sweet souls, they'll scarce give a man leave to be ready; that's their only fault, i'faith: if they be once set upon a thing, why, there's no removing of 'em, till their pretty wills be fulfilled. O, pity thy poor oppressed client here, sweet Cupid, that has scarce six hours' vacation in a month, his causes hang in so many courts, yet never suffer my French adversary, nor his big swoll'n confederates, to overthrow me,
Who without mercy would my blood carouse,

And lay me in prison in a doctor's house.
Thy clemency, great Cupid! Peace, who comes here?

[Enter **PURSENET**.

PURSENET
Sir gallant, well encountered.

TAILBY
I both salute and take my leave together.

PURSENET
Why, whither so fast, sir?

TAILBY
Excuse me, pray;
I'm in a little haste; my horse waits for me.

PURSENET
What, some journey toward?

TAILBY
A light one, i'faith, sir.

PURSENET
I'm sorry that my business so commands me,
I cannot ride with you; but I make no question
You have company enough.

TAILBY
Alas, not any!
[Aside] Nor do I desire it.—Why, 'tis but a Kingston yonder.

PURSENET
O, cry you mercy, sir.

TAILBY
'Scape but one reach,
There's a little danger thither.

PURSENET
True, a little of Combe Park.

TAILBY
You've nam'd the place, sir; that's all I fear, i'faith.

PURSENET
Farewell, sweet Master Tailby.

[Exit **TAILBY**.

This fell out happily;
I'll call this purchase mine before I greet him;
E'en where his fear lies most, there will I meet him.

[Exit.

SCENE II - Combe Park

Enter **PURSENET** with a scarf over his face, and **BOY**.

PURSENET
Boy.

BOY
Sir?

PURSENET
Walk my horse behind yon thicket; give a word if you descry.

BOY
I have all perfect, sir.

[Exit.

PURSENET
So; he cannot now be long. What with my boy's dexterity at ordinaries, and my gelding's celerity over hedge and ditch, but we make pretty shift to rub out a gallant; for I have learnt these principles:
Stoop thou to th' world, 'twill on thy bosom tread;
It stoops to thee, if thou advance thy head.
The mind being far more excellent than fate,
'Tis fit our mind then be above our state.
Why should I write my extremities in my brow,
To make them loathe me that respect me now?
If every man were in his courses known,
Legs that now honour him might spurn him down.
To conclude, nothing seems as it is but honesty, and that makes it so little regarded amongst us.

BOY [Within]
Ela, ha, ho!

PURSENET
The boy? He's hard at hand;
I'll cross him suddenly: and here he comes.

[Enter **TAILBY**.

Stand!

TAILBY
Ha!

PURSENET
Deliver your purse, sir.

TAILBY
I feared none but this place, i'faith; nay, when my mind gives me a thing once—

PURSENET
Quick, quick, sir, quick; I must despatch three robberies yet ere night.

TAILBY
I'm glad you have such good doings, by my troth, sir.

PURSENET
You'll fare ne'er a whit the better for your flattery, I warrant you, sir.

TAILBY
I speak sincerely; 'tis pity such a proper-parted gentleman should want; nor shall you, as long as I have't about me.

[**PURSENET** rifles his pockets.

Nay, search and spare not: there's a purse in my left pocket, as I take it, with fifteen pound in gold in't, and there's a fair chain of pearl in the other: nay, I'll deal truly you; it grieves me, i'faith, when I see such goodly men in distress; I'll rather want it myself than they should go without it.

PURSENET
And that shows a good nature, sir.

TAILBY
Nay, though I say it, I have been always counted a man of a good nature;
I might have hanged myself ere this time else.
Pray, use me like a gentleman; take all,
But injury not my body.

PURSENET
You must pardon me, sir;
I must a little play the usurer,
And bind you, for mine own security.

TAILBY

Alas! There's no conscience in that, sir! Shall
I enter into bond and pay money too?

PURSENET
Tut, I must not be betrayed.

TAILBY
Hear me but what
I say, sir; I do protest I would not be he
That should betray a man, to be prince of the world.

PURSENET
Mass, that's the devil—I thank you heartily—
For he's call'd prince a' th' world.

TAILBY
You take me still at worst.

PURSENET
Swear on this sword then,
To set spurs to your horse, not to look back,
To give no marks to any passenger.

TAILBY
Marks? Why, I think you have left me ne'er a penny, sir.

PURSENET
I mean, no marks of me.

TAILBY
I understand you, sir.

PURSENET
Swear then.

TAILBY
I'faith, I do, sir.

PURSENET
Away!

TAILBY
I'm gone, sir. [Aside] By my troth, of a fierce thief he seems to be a very honest gentleman.

[Exit.

PURSENET
Why, this was well adventur'd, trim a gallant!

Now, with a courteous and long-thirsting eye,
Let me behold my purchase,
And try the soundness of my bones with laughter.
How? Is not this the chain of pearl I gave
To that perjured harlot? 'Tis, 'sfoot, 'tis,
The very chain! O damned mistress! Ha!
And this the purse which, not five days before,
I sent her filled with fair spur-royals? Heart,
The very gold! 'Slife, is this no robbery?
How many oaths flew toward heaven,
Which ne'er came half-way thither, but, like firedrakes,
Mounted a little, gave a crack, and fell:
Feign'd oaths bound up to sink more deep to hell.
What folded paper's this? Death, 'tis her hand!
[Reading] "Master Tailby, you know with what affection I love you." You do? "I count the world but as my prey to maintain you." The more dissembling quean you, I must tell you. "I have sent you an embroidered purse here with fifty fair spur-royals in't." A pox on you for your labour, wench! "And I desire you of all loves to keep that chain of pearl from Master Pursenet's sight." He cannot, strumpet; I behold it now, unto thy secret torture. "So fare thee well, but be constant and want nothing"—as long as I ha't, i'faith, methinks it should have gone so. Well, what a horrible age do we live in, that a man cannot have a quean to himself! Let him but turn his back, the best of her is chipp'd away like a court loaf, that when a man comes himself, has nothing but bumbast; and these are two simple chippings here. Does my boy pick and I steal to enrich myself, to keep her, to maintain him? Why, this is right the sequence of the world. A lord maintains her, she maintains a knight, he maintains a whore, she maintains a captain. So in like manner the pocket keeps my boy, he keeps me, I keep her, she keeps him; it runs like quicksilver from one to another. 'Sfoot, I perceive I have been the chief upholder of this gallant all this while: it appears true, we that pay dearest for our pasture are ever likely worse used. 'Sfoot, he has a nag can run for nothing, has his choice, nay, and gets by the running of her. O fine world, strange devils, and pretty damnable affections!

BOY [Within]
Lela, ha, ho!

PURSENET
There, boy, again: what news there?

[Enter **BOY**.

BOY
Master, pist, master!

PURSENET
How now, boy?

BOY
I have descried a prize.

PURSENET

Another, lad?

BOY
The gull, the scholar.

PURSENET
Master Bouser?

BOY
Ay;
Comes along this way.

PURSENET
Without company?

BOY
As sure as he is your own.

PURSENET
Back to thy place, boy.

[Exit **BOY**.

I have the luck today to rob in safety;
Two precious cowards! Whist; I hear him.

[Enter **FITSGRAVE**.

Stand!

FITSGRAVE
You lie; I came forth to go.

PURSENET
Deliver your purse.

FITSGRAVE
'Tis better in my pocket.

PURSENET
How now? At disputations, signior fool?

FITSGRAVE
I've so much logic to confute a knave,
A thief, a rogue!

[Attacks and strikes **PURSENET** down.

PURSENET
Hold, hold, sir, and you be
A gentleman, hold! Let me rise.

FITSGRAVE [Aside]
Heart!
'Tis the courtesy of his scarf unmask'd him to me
Above the lip by chance: I'll counterfeit.—
Light,
Because I am a scholar, you think belike
That scholars have no metal in 'em, but you
Shall find I have not done with you, cousin.

[Beats **PURSENET**.

PURSENET
As you're a gentleman!

FITSGRAVE
As you're a rogue!

PURSENET
Keep on upon your way, sir.

FITSGRAVE
You bade me stand—

PURSENET
I have been once down for that.

FITSGRAVE
And then deliver.

PURSENET
Deliver me from you, sir!
O, pax on't, has wounded me!
Ela, ha, ho: my horse, my horse, boy!

[Exit.

FITSGRAVE
Have you your boy so ready? O thou world,
How art thou muffled in deceitful forms!
There's such a mist of these, and still hath been,
The brightness of true gentry is scarce seen.
This journey was most happily assign'd;
I've found him dross both in his means and mind.
What paper's this he dropp'd? I'll look on't as I go.

[Exit.

SCENE III - Near Combe Park

Enter **PURSENET** and **BOY**.

PURSENET
A gull call you him? Let me always set upon wise men; they'll be afraid of their lives; they have a feeling of their iniquities, and know what 'tis to die with fighting: 'sfoot, this gull lays on without fear or wit. How deep's it, sayst thou, boy?

BOY
By my faith, three inches, sir.

PURSENET
La, this was long of you, you rogue!

BOY
Of me, sir?

PURSENET
Forgive me, dear boy; my wound ached, and I grew angry: there's hope of life, boy, is there not?

BOY
Pooh, my life for yours!

[Exit **BOY**.

PURSENET
A comfortable boy in man's extremes! I was ne'er so afraid in my life but the fool would have seen my face: he had me at such advantage, he might have commanded my scarf. I 'scaped well there; 't 'ad choked me; my reputation had been past recovery: yet live I unsuspected, and still fit for gallant's choice societies. But here I vow, if e'er I see this Bouser when he cannot see me, either in by-lane, privileged place, court, alley or come behind him when he's standing,
Or take him when he reels from a tavern late,
Pissing again a conduit, wall, or gate;
When he's in such a plight, and clear from men,
I'll do that I'm ashamed to speak till then.

[Exit.

SCENE IV - A Street

Enter two **GENTLEMEN, FITSGRAVE** and the **FIRST GENTLEMAN**.

FITSGRAVE
Nay, read forward. I have found three of your gallants, like your bewitching shame, merely sophistical: there's your bawd-gallant, your pocket-gallant, and your whore-gallant.

FIRST GENTLEMAN [Reading]
"Master Tailby—"

FITSGRAVE
That's he.

FIRST GENTLEMAN [Reading]
"I count the world but as my prey to maintain you."

FITSGRAVE
That's just the phrase and style of 'em all to him; they meet altogether in one effect, and it may well hold, too, for they all jump upon one cause, subaudi lechery.

FIRST GENTLEMAN
What shapes can flattery take! Let me entreat you,
Both in the virgin's right and our good hopes,
Since your hours are so fortunate, to proceed.

FITSGRAVE
Why, he's base that fares until he crown his deed.

[Exit with **FIRST GENTLEMAN**.

SCENE V - A Room in Primero's House

Enter **PURSENET** his arm in a scarf and **BOY**, meeting **FIRST COURTESAN**.

PURSENET [Aside]
See that dissembling devil, that perjur'd strumpet!

FIRST COURTESAN
Welcome, my soul's best wish. O, out, alas!
Thy arm bound in a scarf? I shall swoon instantly.

PURSENET
Heart, and I'll fetch you again in the same tune.
O my unmatch'd love, if any spark of life remain,
Look up, my comfort, my delight, my—

FIRST COURTESAN

O good, O good!

PURSENET
The organ of her voice is tun'd again;
There's hope in women when their speech returns;
See, like the moon after a black eclipse,
She by degrees recovers her pure light.
How cheers my love?

FIRST COURTESAN
As one new-wak'd out of a deadly trance,
The fit scarce quiet.

PURSENET
'Twas terrible for the time;
I'd much ado to fetch you.

FIRST COURTESAN [Aside]
'Shrew your fingers!—
How came my comfort wounded? Speak.

PURSENET
Faith, in a fray last night.

FIRST COURTESAN
In a fray? Will you lose your blood so vainly?
Many a poor creature lacks it. Tell me, how?
What was the quarrel?

PURSENET
Loath to tell you that.

FIRST COURTESAN
Loath to tell me?

PURSENET
Yet 'twas my cause of coming.

FIRST COURTESAN
Why, then, must not I know it?

PURSENET
Since you urge it,
You shall: you're a strumpet!

FIRST COURTESAN
O, news abroad, sir!

PURSENET
Say you so?

FIRST COURTESAN
Why, you knew that the first night you lay with me.

PURSENET
Nay, not to me only, but to the world.

FIRST COURTESAN
Speak within compass, man.

PURSENET
Faith, you know none,
You sail without.

FIRST COURTESAN
I have the better skill then.

PURSENET
At my first step into a tavern-room, to spy
That chain of pearl wound on a stranger's arm
You begg'd of me!

FIRST COURTESAN
How? You mistook it sure.

PURSENET
By heaven, the very self-same chain!

FIRST COURTESAN
O, cry you mercy, 'tis true, I'd forgot it: 'tis Saint George's day tomorrow: I lent it to my cousin only to grace his arm before his mistress.

PURSENET
Notable cunning!

FIRST COURTESAN
And is this all now, i'faith?

PURSENET
Not; I durst go further.

FIRST COURTESAN
Why, let me never possess your love if you see not that again a' Thursday morning: I take't unkindly, i'faith, you should fall out with me for such a trifle.

PURSENET

Better and better!

FIRST COURTESAN
Come, a kiss, and friends!

PURSENET
Away!

FIRST COURTESAN
By this hand, I'll spoil your arm and you will not.

PURSENET
More for this than the devil—

[Enter **GOLDSTONE, TAILBY, FITSGRAVE, BUNGLER,** and **COURTESANS**.

GOLDSTONE
Yea, at your book so hard?

PURSENET
Against my will. [Aside] Are you there, Signior Logic? A pox of you, sir!

GOLDSTONE
Why, how now? What has fate sent us here, in the name of Venus, goddess of Cyprus?

PURSENET
A freebooter's pink, sir, three or four inches deep.

GOLDSTONE
No more? That's conscionable, i'faith.

TAILBY
Troth, I'm sorry for't: pray, how came it, sir?

PURSENET
Faith, by a paltry fray, in Coleman Street.

FITSGRAVE [Aside]
Combe Park, he would say.

PURSENET
No less than three at once, sir,
Made a triangle with their swords and daggers,
And all opposing me.

FITSGRAVE
And amongst those three only one hurt you, sir?

PURSENET
Ex for ex.

TAILBY
Troth, and I'll tell you what luck I had too, since I parted from you last.

PURSENET
What, I pray?

TAILBY
The day you offered to ride with me, I wish now I'd had your company: 'sfoot, I was set upon in Combe Park by three too.

PURSENET
Bah!

TAILBY
Robbed, by this light, of as much gold and jewels as I value at forty pound.

PURSENET
Sure Saturn is in the fifth house.

TAILBY
I know not that; he may be in the sixth and he will for me: I am sure they were in my pocket wheresoever they are; but I'll ne'er refuse a gentleman's company again when 'tis offered me, I warrant you.

GOLDSTONE
I must remember you 'tis Mitre-night, ladies.

SECOND COURTESAN
Mass, 'tis indeed Friday today, I'd quite forgot: when a woman's busy, how the time runs away!

FIRST COURTESAN [Taking **TAILBY** aside]
O, you've betrayed us both!

TAILBY
I understand you not.

FIRST COURTESAN
You've let him see the chain of pearl I gave you.

TAILBY
Who? Him? Will you believe me, by this hand,
He never saw it.

FIRST COURTESAN
Upon a stranger's arm he swore to me.

TAILBY
Mass, that may be; for the truth is, i'faith,
I was robb'd on't at Combe Park.

FIRST COURTESAN
'Twas that betrayed it.

TAILBY
I would I had stay'd him;
He was no stranger, he was a thief, i'faith,
For thieves will be no strangers.

FIRST COURTESAN
How shall I excuse it?

[**BUNGLER** seizes the **BOY**, who had attempted to pick his pocket.

BUNGLER
Nay, I have you fast enough, boy; you rogue!

BOY
Good sir, I beseech you, sir, let me go!

BUNGLER
A pickpocket! Nay, you shall to Newgate, look you. [To **PURSENET**] Is this your boy, sir?

PURSENET
How now, boy? A monster? Thy arm lined fast in another's pocket? Where learnt you that manners? What company have you kept a' late, that you are so transformed into a rogue? That shape I know not. Believe me, sir, I much wonder at the alteration of this boy, where he should get this nature: as good a child to see to, and as virtuous; he has his creed by heart, reads me his chapter duly every night; he will not miss you one tittle in the nine commandments.

BUNGLER
There's ten of 'em.

PURSENET
I fear he skips o'er one, "Thou shalt not steal."

BUNGLER
Mass, like enough.

PURSENET
Else grace and memory would quite abash the boy.
[To **BOY**] Thou graceless imp! Ah, thou prodigious child,
Begot at some eclipse, degenerate rogue,
Shame to thy friends, and to thy master eke!

How far digressing from the noble mind
Of thy brave ancestors, that lie in marble
With their coat-armours o'er 'em!

BUNGLER
Had he such friends?

PURSENET
The boy is well descended, though he be a rogue, and has no feeling on't; yet for my sake, and for my reputation's, seek not the blood of the boy; he's near allied to many men of worship now yet living; a fine old man to his father; it would kill his heart, i'faith; he'd away like a chrisom.

BUNGLER
Alas, good gentleman!

PURSENET
Ah, shameless villain,
Complain'st thou? Dost thou want?

BOY
No, no, no, no!

PURSENET
Art not well clad? Thy hunger well resisted?

BOY
Yes, yes, yes, yes!

PURSENET
But thou shall straight to Bridewell.

BOY
Sweet master!

PURSENET
Live upon bread and water and chap-choke.

BOY
I beseech your worship!

BUNGLER [Taking **PURSENET** aside]
Come, I'll be his surety for once.

PURSENET
You shall excuse me indeed, sir.

BUNGLER

He will mend: 'a may prove an honest man for all this. I know gallant gentlemen now that have done as much as this comes to in their youth.

PURSENET
Say you so, sir?

BUNGLER
And as for Bridewell, that will but make him worse; 'a will learn more knavery there in one week than will furnish him and his heirs for a hundred year.

PURSENET
Deliver the boy!

BUNGLER
Nay, I tell you true, sir; there's none goes in there a quean, but she comes out an arrant whore, I warrant you.

PURSENET
The boy comes not there for a million!

BUNGLER
No, you had better forgive him by ten parts.

PURSENET
True; but 'a must not know it comes from me.
[To **BOY**] Down a' your knees, you rogue,
And thank this gentleman has got your pardon.

BOY
O, I thank your worship!

PURSENET [Aside to **BOY**] A pox on you for a rogue;
You put me to my set speech once a quarter.

GOLDSTONE
Nay, gentlemen, you quite forget your hour; lead, Master Bouser.

[Exeunt all but **GOLDSTONE** and **SECOND COURTESAN**.

SECOND COURTESAN
Let me go: you're a dissembler.

GOLDSTONE
How?

SECOND COURTESAN
Did not you promise me a new gown?

GOLDSTONE
Did I not? Yes, faith, did I, and thou shalt have it. [To one offstage] Go, sirrah, run for a tailor presently.

[Enter **TAILOR**.

Let me see for the colour now: orange-tawny, peach colour. What sayst to a watchet satin?

SECOND COURTESAN
O, 'tis the only colour I affect!

TAILOR
A very orient colour, an't please your worships. I made a gown on't for a gentlewoman t'other day, and it does passing well upon her.

GOLDSTONE
A watchet satin gown—

TAILOR
There your worship left, sir.

GOLDSTONE
Laid about, tailor.

TAILOR
Very good, sir.

GOLDSTONE
With four fair laces.

TAILOR
That will be costly, sir.

GOLDSTONE
How, you rogue, costly? Out a' th' house, you slipshod, sham-legged, brown-thread-penny-skeined rascal!

SECOND COURTESAN
Nay, my sweet love—

[Exit **TAILOR**.

GOLDSTONE
Hang him, rogue! He's but a botcher neither: come, I'll send thee a fellow worth a hundred of this, if the slave were clean enough.

[Exeunt.

ACT IV

SCENE I - Before Tailby's Lodging

Enter a **SERVANT** bringing in a suit of satin, who knocks at Tailby's door, from which enter **JACK**.

JACK
Who knocks?

SERVANT
A Christian: pray, is not this Master Tailby's lodging? I was directed hither.

JACK
Yes, this is my master's lodging.

SERVANT
Cry you mercy, sir: is he yet stirring?

JACK
He's awake, but not yet stirring, for he played away half his clothes last night.

SERVANT
My mistress commends her secrets unto him, and presents him by me with a new satin suit here.

JACK
Mass, that comes happily.

SERVANT
And she hopes the fashion will content him.

JACK
There's no doubt to be had of that, sir: your mistress's name, pray?

[**SERVANT** shows **JACK** his mistress's name.

You're much preciously welcome.

SERVANT
I thank you uncommonly, sir.

JACK
The suit shall be accepted, I warrant you, sir.

SERVANT
That's all my mistress desires, sir.

JACK
Fare you well, sir.

SERVANT
Fare you well, sir.

[Exit.

JACK
This will make my master leap out of the bed for joy, and dance Wigmore's galliard in his shirt about the chamber!

[Exit into the house.

SCENE II - A Hall in Tailby's Lodging

The music plays on awhile, then enter **TAILBY**, his man **JACK** after, trussing him.

TAILBY
Came this suit from Mistress Cleveland?

JACK
She sent it secretly, sir.

TAILBY
A pretty requiteful squall! I like that woman that can remember a good turn three months after the date; it shows both a good memory and a very feeling spirit.

JACK
This came fortunately, sir, after all your ill luck last night.

TAILBY
I'd beastly casting, Jack.

JACK
O abominable, sir! You had the scurviest hand; the old serving-man swooped up all.

TAILBY
I am glad the fortune lighted upon the poor fellow, by my troth; it made his master mad.

JACK
Did you mark that, sir? I warrant he has the doggedest master of any poor fellow under the dog-sign: I'd rather serve your worship, I'll say that behind your back, sir, for nothing, as indeed I have no standing wages at all, your worship knows.

TAILBY
O, but your vails, Jack, your vails considered, when you run to and fro between me and mistresses—

JACK
I must confess my vails are able to keep an honest man, go I where I list.

TAILBY
Go to then, Jack.

JACK
But those vails stand with the state of your body, sir, as long as you hold up your head: if that droop once, farewell you, farewell I, farewell all; and droop it will, though all the caudles in Europe should put to their helping hands to't: 'tis e'en as uncertain as playing, now up and now down; for if the bill down rise to above thirty, here's no place for players; so if your years rise to above forty, there's no room for old lechers.

TAILBY
And that's the reason all rooms are taken up for young templars.

JACK
You're in the right, sir.

TAILBY
Pize on't, I pawned a good beaver hat to Master Frip last night, Jack: I feel the want of it now.

[Knocking within.

Hark, who's that knocks?

[Enter a **SERVANT**, bringing in a letter and a beaver hat.

SERVANT
Is Master Tailby stirring?

JACK
What's your pleasure with him? He walks here i' th' hall.

SERVANT
Give your worship good morrow.

TAILBY
Welcome, honest lad.

SERVANT
A letter from my mistress.

TAILBY
Who's thy mistress?

SERVANT
Mistress Newblock.

TAILBY
Mistress Newblock, my sincere love; how does she?

SERVANT
Faith, only ill in the want of your sight.

TAILBY
Alas, dear sweet! I've had such business, I protest I ne'er stood still since I saw her.

SERVANT
She has sent your worship a beaver hat here, with a band best in fashion.

TAILBY
How shall I requite this dear soul?

SERVANT
'Tis not a thing fit for me to tell you, sir, for I have three years to serve yet: your worship knows how, I warrant you.

TAILBY
I know the drift of her letter; and for the beaver, say I accept it highly.

SERVANT
O, she will be a proud woman of that, sir!

TAILBY
And hark thee; tell thy mistress, as I'm a gentleman, I'll despatch her out of hand the first thing I do, a' my credit: canst thou remember these words now?

SERVANT
Yes, sir; as you are a gentleman, you'll despatch her out of hand the first thing you do.

TAILBY
Ay, a' my credit.

SERVANT
O, of your credit; I thought not of that, sir.

TAILBY
Remember that, good boy.

SERVANT
Fear it not now, sir.

[Exit.

TAILBY

I dreamt tonight, Jack, I should have a secret supply out a' th' city.

JACK
Your dream crawls out partly well, sir.

[Enter a **SERVANT**, bringing in a purse.

What news there now?

SERVANT
I have an errand to Master Tailby.

JACK
Yonder walks my master.

SERVANT
Mistress Tiffany commends her to your worship, and has sent you your ten pound in gold back again, and says she cannot furnish you of the same lawn you desire till after Allhollandtide.

TAILBY
Thank her she would let me understand so much.

[Exit **SERVANT**.

Ha, ha!
This wench will live: why, this was sent like a
Workwoman now; the rest are botchers to her.
Faith, I commend her cunning: she's a fool
That makes her servant fellow to her heart;
It robs her of respect, dams up all duty,
Keeps her in awe e'en of the slave she keeps:
This takes a wise course—I commend her more—
Sends back the gold I never saw before.
Well, women are my best friends still, i'faith.
Take lands: give me
Good legs, firm back, white hand, black eye, brown hair,
And add but to these five a comely stature;
Let others live by art, and I by nature.

[Exeunt.

SCENE III - A Room with a Door Opening into Fitsgrave's Chamber

Enter **GOLDSTONE**.

GOLDSTONE

Master Bouser, Master Bouser! Ha, ha, ho! Master Bouser!

FITSGRAVE [Within]
Holla!

GOLDSTONE
What, not out of thy kennel, Master Bouser?

FITSGRAVE [Within]
Master Goldstone? You're an early gallant, sir.

GOLDSTONE [Aside]
A fair cloak yonder, i'faith.—By my troth, a-bed, Master Bouser? You remember your promise well o'ernight!

FITSGRAVE [Within]
Why, what's a' clock, sir?

GOLDSTONE
Do you ask that now? Why, the chimes are spent at Saint Bride's.

FITSGRAVE [Within]
'Tis a gentleman's hour: faith, Master Goldstone, I'll be ready in a trice.

GOLDSTONE
Away, there's no trust to you.

FITSGRAVE [Within]
Faith, I'll come instantly.

GOLDSTONE [Aside]
Nay, choose whether you will or no, by my troth, your cloak shall go before you.

[Takes Fitsgrave's cloak.]

FITSGRAVE [Within]
Nay, Master Goldstone, I ha' sworn: do you hear, sir?

GOLDSTONE
Away, away! Faith, I'm angry with you: pox, a-bed now! I'm ashamed of it.

[Exit. As **GOLDSTONE** goes out, **FITSGRAVE** enters in his shirt.

FITSGRAVE
Foot, my cloak, my cloak, Master Goldstone! 'Slife, what mean you by this, sir? You'll bring it back again, I hope. No? Not yet? By my troth, I care very little for such kind of jesting: methinks this familiarity now extends a little too far, unless it be a new fashion come forth this morning secretly; yesterday 'twould have shown unmannerly and saucily. I scarce know yet what to think on't. Well, there's no great profit in

standing in my shirt, I'll on with my clothes: h'as bound me to follow the suit: my cloak's a stranger; he was made but yesterday, and I do not love to trust him alone in company.

[Exit.

SCENE IV - A Street

Enter **FRIPPERY**, wearing Fitsgrave's cloak.

FRIPPERY
What may I conjecture of this Goldstone? He has not only pawned to me this cloak, but the very diamond and sapphire which I bestowed upon my new love at Master Primero's house: the cloak's new, and comes fitly to do me great grace at a wedding this morning, to which I was solemnly invited. I can continue change more than the proudest gallant of 'em all, yet never bestow penny of myself, my pawns do so kindly furnish me: but the sight of these jewels is able to cloy me, did I not preserve my stomach the better for the wedding-dinner. A gift could never have come in a more patient hour, nor to be better desgested. Is she proved false? But I'll not fret today nor chafe my blood.

[Enter **PURSENET**.

PURSENET
Ha! Yonder goes Bouser: the place is fit. [Calling out to **BOY** within] Boy, stand with my horse at corner.

[Attacking **FRIPPERY**

I owe you for a pink three inches deep, sir.

FRIPPERY
O-O-O!

PURSENET
Take that in part of payment for Combe Park.

[Exit.

FRIPPERY
O-O-O!

[Enter **FITSGRAVE**.

FITSGRAVE
How now, who's this? 'Sfoot, one of our gallants knocked down like a calf! Is there such a plague of 'em here at London, they begin to knock 'em a' th' head already?

FRIPPERY
O Master Bouser! Pray, lend me your hand, sir; I am slain!

FITSGRAVE
Slain and alive? O cruel execution!
What man so savage-spirited durst presume
To strike down satin on two taffetas cut,
Or lift his hand against a beaver hat?

FRIPPERY
Some rogue that owes me money, and had no other means. To a wedding-dinner! I must be dressed myself, methinks.

FITSGRAVE
How? Why, this is my cloak: life, how came my cloak hither?

FRIPPERY
Is it yours, sir? Master Goldstone pawned it to me this morning fresh and fasting, and borrowed five pound upon't.

FITSGRAVE
How, pawned it? Pray, let me hear out this story: come, and I'll lead you to the next barber-surgeon's. Pawned my cloak?

[Exit leading out **FRIPPERY**.

SCENE V - Another Street]

Enter **BUNGLER, GOLDSTONE,** and **MARMADUKE**.

BUNGLER
How now, Marmaduke? What's the wager?

MARMADUKE
Nay, my care is at end, sir, now I am come to the sight of you. My mistress, your cousin, entreats you to take part of a dinner with her at home at her house, and bring what gentleman you please to accompany you.

BUNGLER
Thank my sweet coz: I'll munch with her, say.

MARMADUKE
I'll tell her so.

BUNGLER
Marmaduke—

MARMADUKE

Sir?

BUNGLER
Will there be any stockfish, thinkest thou?

MARMADUKE
How, sir?

BUNGLER
Tell my coz I've a great appetite to stockfish, i'faith.

[Exit **MARMADUKE**.

Master Goldstone, I'll entreat you to be the gentleman that shall accompany me.

GOLDSTONE
Not me, sir?

BUNGLER
You, sir.

GOLDSTONE
By my troth, concluded. What state bears thy coz, sirrah?

BUNGLER
O, a fine merchant's wife.

GOLDSTONE
Or rather, a merchant's fine wife.

BUNGLER
Trust me, and that's the properer phrase here at London; and 'tis as absurd too to call him fine merchant, for, being at sea, a man knows not what pickle he is in.

GOLDSTONE
Why, true.

BUNGLER
Yet my coz will be served in plate, I can tell you; she has her silver jugs and her gilt tankards.

GOLDSTONE
Fie!

BUNGLER
Nay, you shall see a house dressed up, i'faith; you must not think to tread a' th' ground when you come there.

GOLDSTONE

No? How then?

BUNGLER
Why, upon paths made of fig-frails and white blankets cut out in steaks.

GOLDSTONE
Away! [Aside] I have thought of a device.—Where shall we meet an hour hence?

BUNGLER
In Paul's.

GOLDSTONE
Agreed.

[Exit **BUNGLER**. Enter **FITSGRAVE**.

FITSGRAVE
The broker-gallant and the cheating-gallant:
Now I have found 'em all, I so rejoice,
That the redeeming of my cloak I weigh not.
I have spied him.

GOLDSTONE
Pax, here's Bouser.

FITSGRAVE
Master Goldstone, my cloak! Come, where's my cloak, sir?

GOLDSTONE
O, you're a sure gentleman, especially if a man stand in need of you! He may be slain in a morning to breakfast ere you vouchsafe to peep out of your lodging.

FITSGRAVE
How?

GOLDSTONE
No less than four gallants, as I'm a gentleman, drew all upon me at once, and opposed me so spitefully, that I not only lost your cloak i' th' fray—

FITSGRAVE
Comes it in there?

GOLDSTONE
But my rich hangers, sirrah; I think thou hast seen 'em.

FITSGRAVE
Never, i'faith, sir.

GOLDSTONE
Those with the two unicorns, all wrought in pearl and gold: pox on't, it frets me ten times more than the loss of the paltry cloak: prithee, and thou lovest me, speak no more on't; it brings the unicorns into my mind, and thou wouldst not think how the conceit grieves me. I will not do thee that disgrace, i'faith, to offer thee any satisfaction, for in my soul I think thou scornest it; thou bearest that mind, in my conscience; I have always said so of thee. Fare thee well: when shall I see thee at my chamber, when?

FITSGRAVE
Every day, shortly.

GOLDSTONE
I have fine toys to show thee.

FITSGRAVE
You win my heart then.

[Exit **GOLDSTONE**.

The devil scarce knew what a portion he gave his children when he allowed 'em large impudence to live upon, and so turned 'em into th' world: surely he gave away the third part of the riches of his kingdom; revenues are but fools to't.
The filed tongue and the undaunted forehead
Are mighty patrimonies, wealthier than those
The city-sire or the court-father leaves:
In these behold it: riches oft, like slaves,
Revolt; they bear their foreheads to their graves.
What soonest grasps advancement, mends great suits,
Trips down rich widows, gains repute and name,
Makes way where'er it comes, bewitches all?
Thou, Impudence, the minion of our days,
On whose pale cheeks favour and fortune plays.
Call you these your five gallants?
Trust me, they're rare fellows:
They live on nothing; many cannot live on something:
Here they may take example. Suspectless virgin,
How easy had thy goodness been beguil'd!
Now only rests, that as to me they're known
So to the world their base arts may be shown.

[Exit.

SCENE VI - The Middle Aisle of St. Paul's

Enter **PURSENET** and **BOY**.

PURSENET

Art sure thou sawest him receive't, boy?

BOY
Forty pound in gold, as I'm a gentleman born.

PURSENET
Thy father gave the ram's head, boy?

BOY
No, you're deceiv'd; my mother gave that, sir.

PURSENET
What's thy mother's is thy father's.

Enter **PYAMONT**.

BOY
I'm sorry it holds in the ram's head. See, here he walks; I was sure he came into Paul's: the gold had been yours, master, long ere this, but that he wears both his hands in his pockets.

PURSENET
How unfortunately is my purpose seated! What the devil should come in his mind to keep in his hands so long? The biting but of a paltry louse would do me great kindness now; I'd know not how to requite it: will no rascal creature assist me? Stay, what if I did impudently salute 'em out? Good. Boy, be ready, boy.

BOY
Upon the least advantage, sir.

PURSENET [To **PYAMONT**]
You're most devoutly met in Paul's, sir.

PYAMONT
So are you, but I scarce remember you, sir.

PURSENET
O, I cry you mercy, sir; I pray, pardon me; I fear I have tendered an offence, sir: troth, I took you at the first for one Master Dumpling, a Norfolk gentleman.

[While **PURSENET** speaks, the **BOY** watches in vain for an opportunity to pick Pyamont's pocket.]

PYAMONT
There's no harm done yet, sir.

PURSENET [Aside]
I hope he is there by this time.—How now, boy, hast it?

BOY

No, by troth, have I not; this labour's lost: 'tis in the right pocket, and he kept that hand in sure enough.

PURSENET [Aside]
Unpractised gallant! Salute me but with one hand,
Like a counterfeit soldier? O times and manners!
Are we grown beasts? Do we salute by halves?
Are not our limbs at leisure? Where's comely nurture?
The Italian kiss, or the French cringe,
With the Polonian waist? Are all forgot?
Then misery follows. Surely fate forbade it:
Had he employ'd but his right hand, I'd had it.

[Enter **BUNGLER**.

It must be an everlasting device, I think, that procures both his hands out at once.

[Exit with **BOY**.

PYAMONT
Do you walk, sir?

BUNGLER
No, I stay a little for a gentleman's coming, too.

PYAMONT
Farewell then, sir: I have forty pound in gold about me, which I must presently send down into the country.

BUNGLER
Fare you well, sir.

[Exit **PYAMONT**.

I wonder Master Goldstone spares my company so long; 'tis now about the navel of the day, upon the belly of noon.

[Enter **GOLDSTONE** and **FULK**, both disguised.

GOLDSTONE [Aside to **FULK**]
See where he walks: be sure you let off at a twinkling, now.

FULK [Aside to **GOLDSTONE**]
When did I miss you?—Your worship has forgot you promised Mistress Newcut, your cousin, to dine with her this day.

GOLDSTONE
Mass, that was well remembered.

BUNGLER
I am bold to salute you, sir.

GOLDSTONE
Sir?

BUNGLER
Is Mistress Newcut your cousin, sir?

GOLDSTONE
Yes, she's a cousin of mine, sir.

BUNGLER
Then I am a cousin of yours, by the sister's side.

GOLDSTONE
Let me salute you then; I shall be glad of your farther acquaintance.

BUNGLER
I am a bidden guest there too.

GOLDSTONE
Indeed, sir!

BUNGLER
Faith, invited this morning.

GOLDSTONE
Your good company shall be kindly embraced, sir.

BUNGLER
I walk a turn or two here for a gentleman, but I think he'll either overtake me, or be before me.

GOLDSTONE
'Tis very likely, sir. [To **FULK**] There, sirrah, go to dinner and about two wait for me.

BUNGLER
Nay, let him come between two and three, cousin, for we love to sit long at dinner i' th' city.

GOLDSTONE
Come, sweet cousin.

BUNGLER
Nay, cousin; keep your way, cousin; good cousin, I will not, i'faith, cousin.

[Exeunt.

SCENE VII - A Room in Mistress Newcut's House

MARMADUKE is discovered laying the tablecloth. Enter **MISTRESS NEWCUT**.

MISTRESS NEWCUT
Why, how now, sirrah? Upon twelve of the clock, and not the cloth laid yet? Must we needs keep Exchange time still?

MARMADUKE
I am about it, forsooth.

MISTRESS NEWCUT
You're about it, forsooth? You're still about many things, but you ne'er do one well. I am an ass to keep thee in th' house, now my husband's at sea; thou hast no audacity with thee; a foolish, dreaming lad, fitter to be in the garret than in any place else; no grace nor manly behaviour: when didst thou ever come to me but with thy head hanging down? O decheerful 'prentice, uncomfortable servant!

[Exit **MARMADUKE**.

Pray heaven the gull, my cousin, has so much wit left as to bring Master Tailby along with him—my comfort, my delight!—for that was the chiefest cause I did invite him. I bade him bring what gentleman he pleased to accompany him; as far as I durst go: why may he not then make choice of Master Tailby? Had he my wit or feeling he would do't.

[Enter **BUNGLER**, and **GOLDSTONE** disguised.

BUNGLER
Where's my sweet cousin here? Does she lack any guests?

MISTRESS NEWCUT
Ever such guess as you: you're welcome, cousin.

GOLDSTONE
I am rude, lady.

MISTRESS NEWCUT
You're most welcome, sir.

BUNGLER
There will be a gallant here anon, coz; he promised faithfully.

MISTRESS NEWCUT
Who is't? Master Tailby?

BUNGLER
Master Tailby? No, Master Goldstone.

MISTRESS NEWCUT
Master Goldstone? I could think well of that Goldstone were't not for one vild trick he has.

GOLDSTONE
What's that, lady?

MISTRESS NEWCUT
In jest he will pawn his punks for supper.

GOLDSTONE
That's a vild part in him, i'faith, and he my were brother.

MISTRESS NEWCUT
Pray, gentlemen, sit awhile; your dinner shall come presently.

[Exit.

GOLDSTONE [Aside]
Yes, Mistress Newcut? At first give me a trip?
A close bite always asks a secret nip.

BUNGLER
My cousin here is a very kind-natured soul, i'faith, in her humour.

GOLDSTONE
Pooh, you know her not so well as I, coz; I have observed her in all her humours; you ne'er saw her a little waspish, I think.

BUNGLER
I have not, i'faith.

GOLDSTONE
Pooh, then ye ne'er saw pretty humour in your life; I can bring her into't when I list.

BUNGLER
Would you could, i'faith!

GOLDSTONE
Would I could? By my troth, and I were sure thou couldst keep thy countenance, coz, what a pretty jest have I thought upon already to entertain time dinner!

BUNGLER
Prithee, coz, what is't? I love a jest a' life, i'faith.

GOLDSTONE
Ah, but I am jealous you will not keep your countenance, i'faith! Why, ye shall see a pretty story of a humour. Faith, I'll try you for once: you know my cousin will wonder when she comes in to see the cloth laid, and ne'er a salt upon the board.

BUNGLER
That's true, i'faith.

GOLDSTONE
Now will I stand a while out of sight with it, and give her humour play a little.

BUNGLER
Coz, dost thou love me? And thou wilt ever do anything for me, do't.

GOLDSTONE
Marry, I build upon your countenance.

BUNGLER
Why, dost thou think I'm an ass, coz?

GOLDSTONE
I would be loath to undertake it else; for if you should burst out presently, coz, the jest would be spoiled.

BUNGLER
Why, do not I know that? Away, stand close!

[Exit **GOLDSTONE** with the salt-cellar.

So, so; mum, cousin. A merry companion, i'faith: here will be good sport anon. Whist, she comes.

[Enter **MISTRESS NEWCUT**.

MISTRESS NEWCUT
I make you stay long for a bad dinner here, cousin; if Master Goldstone were come, the meat's e'en ready.

BUNGLER
Some great business detains him, cousin, but he'll not be long now.

MISTRESS NEWCUT
Why, how now? Cuds my life!

BUNGLER
Why—

MISTRESS NEWCUT
Was ever mistress so plagued with a shuttle-headed servant! Why, Marmaduke!

[Enter **MARMADUKE**.

MARMADUKE

I come, forsooth.

MISTRESS NEWCUT
Able to shame me from generation to generation!

MARMADUKE
Did you call, forsooth?

MISTRESS NEWCUT
Come hither, forsooth: did you lay this cloth?

MARMADUKE
Yes, forsooth.

MISTRESS NEWCUT
Do you use to lay a cloth without a salt, a salt, a salt, a salt, a salt!

MARMADUKE
How many salts would you have? I'm sure I set the best I' the house upon the board.

BUNGLER
How, cousin? [Singing] "Cousin, cousin, did call, coz?"

MISTRESS NEWCUT
Did you see a salt upon the board when you came in?

BUNGLER
Pooh!

MISTRESS NEWCUT
Come, come, I thought as much; beshrew your fingers, where is't now?

BUNGLER
Your cousin yonder—

MISTRESS NEWCUT
Why, the man's mad!

BUNGLER
Cousin, hist, cousin!

MISTRESS NEWCUT
What say you?

BUNGLER
Pooh, I call not you, I call my cousin. Come forth with the salt, cousin! Ha! How? Nobody? Why, was not he that came in e'en now your cousin?

MISTRESS NEWCUT
My cousin? O my bell-salt, O my great bell-salt!

[Enter **GOLDSTONE** in his own dress.

BUNGLER
The tenor bell-salt. O, here comes Master Goldstone now, cousin; he may tell us some news on him. [To **GOLDSTONE**] Did you not meet a fellow about door with a great silver salt under his arm?

GOLDSTONE
No, sure; I met none such.

MISTRESS NEWCUT
Pardon me, sir, I forgot all this while to bid you welcome. I shall loath this room for ever. Take hence the cloth, you unlucky, maple-faced rascal! Come, you shall dine in my chamber, sir.

GOLDSTONE
No better place, lady.

[Exeunt.

SCENE VIII - A Street

Enter **PYAMONT**.

PYAMONT
No less than forty pound in fair gold at one lift! The next shall swoon and swoon again till the devil fetch him, ere I set hand to him. Heart, nothing vexes me so much, but that I paid the goldsmith for the change too not an hour before: had I let it alone in the chain of silver as it was at first, it might have given me some notice at his departure: 'sfoot, I could fight with a windmill now. Sure 'twas some unlucky villain: why should he come and salute me wrongfully too, mistake me at noonday? Now I think on't in cold blood, it could not be but an induction to some villainous purpose: well, I shall meet him—

[Enter **PURSENET**.

PURSENET
This forty pound came fortunately to redeem my chain of pearl from mortgage: I would not care how often I swooned to have such a good caudle to comfort me; gold and pearl is very restorative.

PYAMONT
See, yonder's the rogue I suspect for foul play! I'll walk muffled by him, offer some offence or cause of a quarrel, only to try his temper; if he be a coward, he's the likelier to be a rogue, an infallible note.

[Jostles **PURSENET**.

PURSENET

What a pox ail you, sir? Would I had been aware of you!

PYAMONT
Sir, speak you to me?

PURSENET
Not I, sir: pray, keep on your way; I have nothing to say to you.

PYAMONT
You're a rascal!

PURSENET
You may say your pleasure, sir; but I hope I go not like a rascal.

PYAMONT
Are you fain to fly to your clothes because you're gallant? Why, there's no rascal like your gallant rascal, believe that.

PURSENET
You have took me at such an hour, faith, you may call me e'en what you please; nothing will move me.

PYAMONT
No? I'll make somewhat move you. Draw! I suspected you were a rogue, and you have purs'd it up well with a coward!

PURSENET
Who, my patron?

PYAMONT
Keep out, you rascal!

PURSENET
The guest that did me the kindness in Paul's? Hold, as you are a gentleman; you'll give me breath, sir?

[Exit running; as he goes out, he drops the chain of pearl.

PYAMONT
Are you there with me? A vengeance stop you! You have found breath enough to run away from me. I will never meet this slave hereafter in a morning, but I will breathe myself upon him; since I can have no other satisfaction, he shall save me that forty pound in fence-school.

[Exit. Enter **GOLDSTONE**.

GOLDSTONE
When things are cleanly carried, sign of judgment:
I was the welcom'st gallant to her alive
After the salt was stolen; then a good dinner,
A fine provoking meal, which drew on apace

The pleasure of a day-bed, and I had it;
This here one ring can witness: when I parted,
Who but "sweet Master Goldstone?"
I left her in that trance. What cannot wit,
So it be impudent, devise and compass?
I'd fain know that fellow now
That would suspect me but for what I am;
He lives not: 'tis all in the conveyance.
What, thou look'st not like a beggar:
What mask'st thou on the ground?
I've a hand to help thee up: a fair chain of pearl!

[Takes up the chain of pearl which **PURSENET** had dropped.

Surely a merchant's wife gives lucky handsel:
They that find pearl may wear't at a cheap rate;
Marry, my lady dropp'd it from her arm
For a device to tole me to her bed:
I've seen as great a matter. Who be these?
I'll be too crafty for you.

[Enter **PRIMERO** and **FRIPPERY**.

O Monsieur Primero, Signior Frip; is it you, gallants?

FRIPPERY
Sweet Master Goldstone!

[They talk apart. Enter **TAILBY** and two **CONSTABLES**.

TAILBY
Every bawd exceeds me in fortune: Master Primero was robbed of a carkanet upon Monday last; laid the goldsmiths, and found it. I ha' laid goldsmith, jeweller, burnisher, broker, and the devil and all, I think, yet could never so much as hear of that chain of pearl: he was a notable thief; he works close. Peace, who be these? Ha, let me see. By this light, there it is! Back, lest they see thee: a happy minute! Goldstone? What an age do we breathe in! Who that saw him now would think he were maintained by purses? So, who that meets me would think I were maintained by wenches? As far as I can see, 'tis all one case, and holds both in one court; we are both maintained by the common roadway! Keep thou thine own heart, thou livest unsuspected. I leese you again now.

GOLDSTONE
But, I pray you, tell me, met you no gentlewomen by the way you came?

FRIPPERY
Not any: what should they be?

GOLDSTONE
Nay, I do but ask, because a gentlewoman's glove was found near to the place I met you.

PRIMERO
Faith, we saw none, sir.

TAILBY
Good officers, upon suspicion of felony.

SECOND CONSTABLE
Very good, sir.

FIRST CONSTABLE
What call you the thief's name you do suspect?

TAILBY
Master Justinian Goldstone.

FIRST CONSTABLE
Remember, Master Justinian Goldstone; a terrible world the whilst, my masters!

TAILBY
Look you, that's he: upon him, officers!

FIRST CONSTABLE
I see him not yet; which is he, sir?

TAILBY
Why, that.

FIRST CONSTABLE
He a thief, sir? Who, that gentleman i' th' satin?

TAILBY
E'en he.

FIRST CONSTABLE
Farewell, sir; you're a merry gentleman.

TAILBY
As you will answer it, officers! I'll bear you out, I'll be your warrant.

FIRST CONSTABLE
Nay, and you say so. What's his name then?

TAILBY
Justinian Goldstone.

[The **CONSTABLES** approach and seize **GOLDSTONE**.

FIRST CONSTABLE
Master Justinian Goldstone, we apprehend you, sir, upon suspicion of felony.

GOLDSTONE
Me?

TAILBY
You, sir.

[**GOLDSTONE** struggles.

SECOND CONSTABLE
I charge you, in the king's name, gentlemen, to assist us.

GOLDSTONE
Master Tailby!

TAILBY
The same man, sir.

GOLDSTONE
Life, what's the news?

TAILBY
Ha' you forgot Combe Park?

GOLDSTONE
Combe Park? No, 'tis in Kingston way.

TAILBY
I believe you'll find it so.

GOLDSTONE
I not deny it.

FIRST CONSTABLE
Bear witness, has confessed.

GOLDSTONE
What have I confessed? Pair of coxcombs indubitable!

TAILBY
I was robb'd finely of this chain of pearl there, and forty fair spur-royals.

GOLDSTONE
Did I rob you?

TAILBY

There where I find my goods I may suspect, sir.

FRIPPERY
I dreamt this would be his end.

GOLDSTONE
See how I am wrong'd, gentlemen: as I've a soul, I found this chain of pearl not three yards from this place, just when I met you.

TAILBY
Ha, ha!

FRIPPERY
Yet the law's such, if he but swear 'tis you, you're gone.

GOLDSTONE
Pox on't, that e'er I saw't!

FRIPPERY
Can you but swear 'tis he? Do but that, and you tickle him, i'faith.

TAILBY
Nay, and it come once to swearing, let me alone.

FRIPPERY
Say, and hold; he called my jewels counterfeit, and so cheated the poor wench of 'em.

FIRST CONSTABLE
Come, bring him away, come.

GOLDSTONE
'Twill call my state in question.

[Enter **PURSENET**.

PURSENET [Aside]
I think what's got by theft doth never prosper;
Now lost my chain of pearl.—Come, Master Goldstone,
Let go this; 'tis mine, i'faith.

GOLDSTONE
The chain of pearl?

PURSENET
By my troth, it's mine.

GOLDSTONE
By my troth, much good do't you, sir.

FRIPPERY
I'm glad in my soul, sir.

FIRST CONSTABLE
Deliver your weapons.

PURSENET
How!

FIRST CONSTABLE
You're apprehended upon suspicion of felony.

PURSENET
Felony! What's that?

TAILBY
Was it you, i'faith, sir, all this while, that did me that kindness to ease both my pockets at Combe Park?

PURSENET
I, sir?
Pray, gentlemen, draw near; let's talk among ourselves.
[To **FIRST CONSTABLE**] Stand apart, scoundrel. [To the **GALLANTS**]
Must every gentleman
Be upbraided in public that flies out
Now and then upon necessity,
To be themes for pedlars and weavers? This should
Not be: 'twas never seen among the Romans,
Nor read we of it in the time of Brute:
Are we more brutish now?
Did I list to blab, do not I know your course
Of life, Master Tailby to be as base
As the basest, maintained by me, by him, by all
Of us, and 'a second-hand from mistresses?
I've their letters here to show.
Why should you be so violent to strip naked
Another's reputation to the world,
Knowing your own so leprous?
Beside, this chain of pearl and those spur-royals
Came to you falsely; for she broke her faith,
And made her soul a strumpet with her body,
When she sent those; they were ever justly mine.
[To **PRIMERO**] Pray, what moves you, sir? Why should you shake your head?
You're clear; sure I should know you, sir: pray, are you not sometimes a pander, and oftener a bawd, sir? Have I never sinned in your banqueting boxes, your bowers and towers? You slave, that keeps fornication upon the tops of trees, the very birds cannot engender in quiet for you! Why, rogue, that goes in good clothes made out of wenches' cast gowns—

PRIMERO
Nothing goes so near my heart as that.

PURSENET
Do you shake your slave's noddle?

TAILBY
And here's a rascal look'st away too—saving the presence of Master Goldstone—a filthy-slimy-lousy-nittical broker, pricked up in pawns from the hat-band to the shoe-string; a necessary hook to hang gentlemen's suits out i' th' air, lest they should grow musty with long lying, which his pawns seldom are guilty of; a fellow of several scents and steams, French, Dutch, Italian, English, and therefore his lice must needs be mongrels: why, bill-money—

GOLDSTONE
I am sorry to hear this among you: you've all deceived me; truly I took you for other spirits. You must pardon me henceforward; I have a reputation to look to; I must be no more seen in your companies.

FRIPPERY
Nay, nay, nay, nay, Master Goldstone, you must not 'scape so, i'faith, one word before you go, sir.

GOLDSTONE
Pray, despatch then; I would not for half my revenues, i'faith, now, that any gallants should pass by in the meantime, and find me in your companies; nay, as quick as you can, sir.

FRIPPERY
You did not take away Master Bouser's cloak t'other morning, pawned it to me, and borrowed five pound upon't?

GOLDSTONE
Ha!

FRIPPERY
'Twas not you neither that finely cheated my little novice at Master Primero's house of a diamond and sapphire, and swore they were counterfeit, both glass, mere glass, as you were a right gentleman?

GOLDSTONE
'Slife, why were we strangers all this while? 'Sfoot, I perceive we are all natural brothers! A pox on's all, are we found, i'faith?

FRIPPERY
A cheater!

GOLDSTONE
A thief, a lecher, a bawd, and a broker!

FIRST CONSTABLE
What mean they to be so merry? I'm afraid they laugh at us, and make fools on's.

GOLDSTONE
Push, leave it to me. [To **FIRST CONSTABLE**] How now, who would you speak withal?

FIRST CONSTABLE
Speak withal! Have we waited all this while for a suspected thief?

GOLDSTONE
How? You're scarce awake yet, I think: look well, does any appear like a thief in this company? Away, you slaves! You stand loitering when you should look to the commonwealth: you catch knaves apace now, do you not? They may walk by your nose, you rascals!

[Exeunt **CONSTABLES**.

ALL
Sweet Master Goldstone!

GOLDSTONE
You lacked spirit in your company till I came among you: here be five on's; let's but glue together, why now the world shall not come between us.

PURSENET
If we be true among ourselves.

GOLDSTONE
Why, true; we cannot lack to be rich, for we cannot lack riches, nor can our wenches want, nor we want wenches.

PRIMERO
Let me alone to furnish you with them.

TAILBY
And me.

GOLDSTONE
There's one care past: and as for the knight's daughter,
Our chiefest business, and least thought upon—

PURSENET
That's true, i'faith.

TAILBY
How shall we agree for her?

GOLDSTONE
With as much ease as for the rest. Tomorrow
Brings the night: let's all appear in the best shape
We may; troth is, we have need on't: and when
Amongst us five she makes election,

As one she shall choose—

PURSENET
True, she cannot but choose.

GOLDSTONE
That one so fortunate amongst us five
Shall bear himself more portly, live regarded,
Keep house, and be a countenance to the rest.

ALL
Admirable!

GOLDSTONE
For instance;
[To **PURSENET** Put case yourself, after some robbery done,
Were pursu'd hardly, why, there were your shelter,
You know your sanctuary; nay, say you were taken,
His letter to the justice will strike't dead:
'Tis policy to receive one for the head.

ALL
Let's hug thee, Goldstone.

GOLDSTONE
What have I begot?

PURSENET
What, sir?

GOLDSTONE
I must plot for you all; it likes me rarely.

TAILBY
Prithee, what is't, sir?

GOLDSTONE
'Twould strike Fitsgrave pale,
And make the other suitors appear blanks.

FRIPPERY
For our united mysteries.

GOLDSTONE
What if we five presented our full shapes
In a strange, gallant and conceited masque?

PURSENET

In a masque? Your thoughts and mine were twins.

TAILBY
So the device were subtle, nothing like it.

FRIPPERY
Some poet must assist us.

GOLDSTONE
Poet?
You'll take the direct line to have us stag'd?
Why, what lacks Bouser? Are you too well, too safe?
An absolute scholar; easy to be wrought,
No danger in the operation.

PURSENET
But have you so much interest?

GOLDSTONE
What, in Bouser?
Why, my least word commands him.

TAILBY
Then no man fitter.

PURSENET
And there's Master Frip, too,
Can furnish us of masquing suits enow.

FRIPPERY
Upon sufficient pawn, I think I can, sir.

PURSENET
Pawn? Jew, here, take my chain: pawns among brothers?
We shall thrive! But we must still expect
One rogue in five, and think us happy, too.

[Enter **FITSGRAVE**.

GOLDSTONE
Last man we spoke on, Master Bouser.

ALL
Little Master Bouser, sweet Master Bouser, welcome, i'faith.

FITSGRAVE
Are your fathers dead, gentlemen, you're so merry?

GOLDSTONE
By my troth, a good jest! Did not I commend his wit to you, gentlemen? Hark, sirrah Ralph Bouser, cousin Bouser, i'faith, there's a kind of portion in town, a girl of fifteen hundred, whom we all powerfully affect, and determine to present our parts to her in a masque.

FITSGRAVE
In a masque.

GOLDSTONE
Right, sir: now, a little of thy brain for a device to present us firm, which we shall never be able to do ourselves, thou knowest that; and with a kind of speech wherein thou mayst express what gallants are, bravely.

FITSGRAVE
Pooh, how can I express 'em otherwise but bravely? Now for a Mercury, and all were fitted.

PURSENET
Could not a boy supply it?

FITSGRAVE
Why, none better.

PURSENET
I have a boy shall put down all the Mercuries i' th' town; 'a will play a Mercury naturally, at his fingers' ends, i'faith.

FITSGRAVE
Why, then we are suited: for torch-bearers and shield-boys, those are always the writer's properties; you're not troubled with them.

GOLDSTONE
Come, my little Bouser, do't finely now, to the life.

FITSGRAVE
I warrant you, gentlemen.

FRIPPERY [Aside to **FITSGRAVE**]
Hist; give me a little touch above the rest, and you can possible, for I mean to present this chain of pearl to her.

FITSGRAVE [Aside to **FRIPPERY**]
Now I know that, let me alone to fit you.

[Exeunt.

ACT V

SCENE I - A Chamber

Enter **COURTESANS** and **MISTRESS NEWCUT**.

FIRST COURTESAN
Come forth, you wary, private whispering strumpet!
Have we found your close haunts,
Your private watch-towers, and your subtle means?

MISTRESS NEWCUT
How then?

SECOND COURTESAN
You can steal secretly hither,
You mystical quean you, at twilight, twitter-lights!
You have a privilege from your hat, forsooth,
To walk without a man, and no suspicion;
But we poor gentlewomen that go in tires
Have no such liberty, we cannot do thus:
Custom grants that to you that's shame in us.

MISTRESS NEWCUT
Have you done yet?

SECOND COURTESAN
You broke the back of one husband already;
And now th' other's dead with grief at sea,
With your secret expenses, close stealths, cunning
Filches, and continued banquets in corners.
Then, forsooth, you must have your milk-baths to white you,
Your roseleaves to sweeten you,
Your bean-flour bags to sleek you, and make you soft,
Smooth, and delicate, for lascivious entertainment

MISTRESS NEWCUT
So, and you think all this while you dance like a thief in a mist, you're safe, nobody can find you! Pray, were not you a feltmonger's daughter at first, that run away with a new courtier for the love of gentlewomen's clothes, and bought the fashion at a dear rate, with the loss of your name and credit? Why, what are all of you but rustical insides and city flesh, the blood of yeomen, and the bum of gentlewomen?

SECOND COURTESAN
What, shall we suffer a changeable forepart out-tongue us? Take that!

[They attack her.

MISTRESS NEWCUT

Murder, murder!

[Enter **FITSGRAVE**.

FITSGRAVE
How now! Why, ladies, a retreat! Come,
You have shown your spirits sufficiently:
You're all land-captains; and so they shall find
That come in your quarters; but have you the law
Free now to fight and scratch among yourselves,
And let your gallants run away with others?

FIRST COURTESAN
How!

SECOND COURTESAN
Good—

FIRST COURTESAN
Sweet Master Bouser!

MISTRESS NEWCUT
Another?

FITSGRAVE
Why then, I perceive you know nothing: why, they are in the way of marriage; a knight's daughter here in town makes her election among 'em this night.

FIRST COURTESAN
This night?

FITSGRAVE
This very night; and they all present themselves in a masque before her: know you not this?

SECOND COURTESAN
O traitor Master Goldstone!

THIRD COURTESAN
Perjured Master Tailby!

MISTRESS NEWCUT
Without soul?

FIRST COURTESAN
She will chase him!

FITSGRAVE
You have more cause to join,

And play the grounds of friendship 'mongst yourselves,
Than rashly run division: I could tell you
A means to pleasure you—

FIRST COURTESAN
Good Master Bouser!

FITSGRAVE
But that you're women, and are hardly secret—

SECOND COURTESAN
We vow it seriously.

FITSGRAVE
You should be all there in presence,
See all, hear all, and yet not they perceive you.

THIRD COURTESAN
So that—

MISTRESS NEWCUT
Sweet Master Bouser, I—

FITSGRAVE
I can
Stand you in stead; for I frame the device.

ALL
If ever—

FITSGRAVE
Will you do't? Hark you— [Whispers.]

FIRST COURTESAN
Content.

SECOND COURTESAN
And I'll make one.

THIRD COURTESAN
And I another:
We'll mar the match.

MISTRESS NEWCUT
When that good news came of my husband's death,
Goldstone promis'd me marriage, and sware to me—

SECOND COURTESAN

I'll bring his oaths in question.

THIRD COURTESAN
So will I.

FITSGRAVE
Agree among yourselves, for shame!

FIRST COURTESAN
Are we
Resolv'd?

SECOND COURTESAN
In this who would not feign?

THIRD COURTESAN
Friends all,
For my part.

MISTRESS NEWCUT
Here's my lip for mine.

THIRD COURTESAN
Round let it go.

SECOND COURTESAN
All wrath thus quench'd.

FIRST COURTESAN
And I conclude it so.

[Exeunt all except **FITSGRAVE**.

FITSGRAVE
How all events strike even with my wishes!
Their own invention damns them.

[Enter two Gentlemen, **PYAMONT**, and **BUNGLER**.

Now, gentlemen,
Stands your assistance firm?

FIRST GENTLEMAN
Why, 'tis our own case;
I'm sorry you should doubt.

SECOND GENTLEMAN
We'll furnish you.

[Enter **PAINTER** with shields.

BUNGLER
Are these our gallants?

FITSGRAVE
Are our gallants these?

PAINTER
Here be five shields, sir.

FITSGRAVE
Finished already? That's well: I'll see thy master shortly.

PAINTER
I'm satisfied.

[Exit.

PYAMONT
Prithee, let's see, Master Fitsgrave.

FITSGRAVE
I have blazed them.

FIRST GENTLEMAN
What's this?

SECOND GENTLEMAN
Fooh, you should be a gallant too, for you're no university scholar.

FITSGRAVE
Look, this is Pursenet; the device, a purse wide open, and the mouth downward: the word, Alienis ecce crumensis!

FIRST GENTLEMAN
What's that?

FITSGRAVE
"One that lives out of other men's pockets."

PYAMONT
That's right!

FITSGRAVE
Here's Goldstone's, three silver dice.

FIRST GENTLEMAN
They run high, two cinques and a quater!

FITSGRAVE
They're high-men, fit for his purpose; the word, Fratremque patremque.

SECOND GENTLEMAN
Nay, he will cheat his own brother; nay, his own father, i'faith!

FITSGRAVE
So much the word imports. Master Primero.

BUNGLER
Pox, what says he now?

FITSGRAVE
The device, an unvalued pearl hid in a cave; the word, Occultos vendit honores.

FIRST GENTLEMAN
What's that?

FITSGRAVE
"One that sells maidenheads by wholesale."

SECOND GENTLEMAN
Excellently proper!

FITSGRAVE
Master Frip.

SECOND GENTLEMAN
That Pythagorical rascal! In a gentleman's suit today, in a knight's tomorrow.

FITSGRAVE
The device for him, a cuckoo sitting on a tree the word, En avis ex avibus, "one bird made of many!" For you know as the sparrow hatches the cuckoo, so the gentleman feathers the broker.

FIRST GENTLEMAN
Let me admire thee, Master Fitsgrave!

FITSGRAVE
They will scorn, gentlemen; and to assist them the better, Pursenet's boy, that little precious pickpocket, has a compendious speech in Latin, and, like a Mercury, presents their dispositions more liberally.

FIRST GENTLEMAN
Never were poor gallants so abused.

FITSGRAVE

Hang 'em! They're counterfeits;
No honest spirit will pity 'em. This is my crown;
So good men smile, I dread no rascal's frown.
Away, bestow yourselves secretly o'erhead;
This is the place appointed for the rehearsal,
To practise their behaviours.

FIRST GENTLEMAN
We are vanish'd.

[Exeunt the two Gentlemen, **PYAMONT**, and **BUNGLER**, who hide themselves above. Enter **GOLDSTONE**, **PURSENET, TAILBY, FRIPPERY, PRIMERO**, and **BOY**.

GOLDSTONE
Master Bouser.

PURSENET
Well said, i'faith; off with your cloaks, gallants; let's fall roundly to our business.

TAILBY
Is the boy perfect?

FITSGRAVE
That's my credit, sir, I warrant you.

FRIPPERY
If our little Mercury should be out, we should scarce be known what we are.

FITSGRAVE
I have took a course for that, fear it not, sir. Look you, first, here be your shields.

GOLDSTONE
Ay, where be our shields?

PURSENET
Which is mine?

TAILBY
Which is mine, Master Bouser? This?

FITSGRAVE
I pray, be contained a little, gentlemen; they'll come all time enough to you, I warrant.

PURSENET
This Frip is grown so violent!

FITSGRAVE
Yours to begin withal, sir.

PURSENET
Well said, Master Bouser!

FITSGRAVE
First the device, a fair purse wide open, the mouth downward; the word, Alienis ecce crumenis!

PURSENET
What's that, prithee?

FITSGRAVE
"Your bounty pours itself forth to all men."

PURSENET
And so it does, i'faith; that's all my fault, bountiful.

FITSGRAVE
Master Goldstone, here's yours, sir; three silver dice; the word, Fratremque patremque.

GOLDSTONE
And what's that?

FITSGRAVE
"Fortune of my side."

GOLDSTONE
Well said, little Bouser, i'faith!

TAILBY
What say you to me, sir?

FITSGRAVE
For the device, a candle in a corner; the word, Consumptio victis.

TAILBY
The meaning of that, sir?

FITSGRAVE
"My light is yet in darkness till I enjoy her."

TAILBY
Right, sir.

PRIMERO
Now mine, sir?

FITSGRAVE
The device, an unvalued pearl hid in a cave.

PRIMERO
Aha, sirs!

FITSGRAVE
The word, Occultos vendit honores.

PRIMERO
Very good, I warrant.

FITSGRAVE
"A black man's a pearl in a fair lady's eye."

PRIMERO
I said 'twas some such thing.

FRIPPERY
My turn must need come now: am I fitted, Master Bouser?

FITSGRAVE
Trust to me: your device here is a cuckoo sitting on a tree.

FRIPPERY
The Welsh leiger; good.

FITSGRAVE
The word, En avis ex avibus!

FRIPPERY
Ay, marry, sir.

FITSGRAVE
Why, do you know what 'tis, sir?

FRIPPERY
No, by my troth, not yet, sir.

FITSGRAVE
O! "I keep one tune, I recant not."

FRIPPERY
I'm like the cuckoo in that indeed: where I love, I hold.

FITSGRAVE
Did I not promise you I would fit you?

GOLDSTONE

They're all very well done, i'faith, and very scholarlike, though I say't before thy face, little Bouser; but I would not have thee proud on't now: come, if this be performed well—

PURSENET
Who, the boy? He has performed deeper matters than this.

PYAMONT [Aside]
Ay, a pox on him! I think was in my pocket now, and truth were known.

BUNGLER [Aside]
I caught him once in mine.

FITSGRAVE
Suppose the shields are presented, then you begin, boy.

BOY
I representing Mercury, am a pickpocket, and have his part at my fingers' ends: "Page I am to that great and secret thief, magno illo et secreto latroni—"

FITSGRAVE
There you make your honour, sir.

BOY
At latroni?

FITSGRAVE
You have it, sir.

PURSENET
Latroni, that's mine.

FITSGRAVE [Aside]
He confesses the thief's his.

PURSENET
Remember, boy, you point latroni to me.

BOY
To you, master.

FITSGRAVE
Proceed.

BOY
"These four are his companions; the one a notable cheater, that will cozen his own father—"

FITSGRAVE
Master Goldstone.

GOLDSTONE
Let me alone, Master Bouser; I can take mine own turn.

FITSGRAVE
Why—

GOLDSTONE
Peace.

BOY
"The second a notorious lecher, maintained by harlots, cujus virtus consumptio corpus."

TAILBY
That's I, Master Bouser.

FITSGRAVE
There you remember your honour, sir.

BOY
"Ille leno pretiosissimus, virgineos ob lucrum vendens honores."

PURSENET
It sounds very well, i'faith.

BOY
"Postremus ille, quamvis apparatu splendidus, is no other than a broker; these feathers are not his own, sed avis ex avibus: all which to be nothing but truth will appear by the event."

FITSGRAVE
I'faith, here's all now, gentlemen.

GOLDSTONE
Short and pithy.

TAILBY
A good boy, i'faith, and a pregnant!

PURSENET
I dare put trust in the boy, sir. [To **BOY**] Forget not, sirrah, at any hand, to point that same latroni to me.

BOY
I warrant you, master.

GOLDSTONE
Come, gentlemen, the time beckons us away.

FITSGRAVE

Ay, furnish, gentlemen, furnish.

PURSENET
Hark, one word, Master Bouser: what's the same latroni? I have a good mind to that word, i'faith.

FITSGRAVE
Latroni? Why, "shrieve of the shire."

PURSENET
I'faith, and I have shriven some shires in my days.

[Exeunt **GOLDSTONE, PURSENET, TAILBY, FRIPPERY, PRIMERO**, and **BOY**.

FITSGRAVE
Now, gentlemen, are you satisfied and pleas'd?

FIRST GENTLEMAN
Never more amply.

FITSGRAVE
Amongst us now falls that desired lot,
For we shall blast five rivals with one plot.

[Exeunt.

SCENE III - A Hall in Katherine's House

Enter **KATHERINE** between two ancient **GENTLEMEN**.

KATHERINE
Grave gentlemen, in whose approved bosoms
My deceas'd father did repose much faith,
You're dearly welcome: pray, sit, command music;
See nothing want to beautify this night,
That holds my election in her peaceful arms;
Feasts, music, hymns, those sweet celestial charms.

FIRST GENTLEMAN
May you be blest in this election.

SECOND GENTLEMAN
That content may meet perfection.

HYMN
Sound lute, bandora gittern,
Viol, virginals, and cittern;

Voices spring, and lift aloud
Her name that makes the music proud!
This night perfection
Makes her election.
Follow, follow, follow, follow round,
Look you to that, nay, you to that, nay, you to that:
Anon you will be found, anon you will be found, anon you will be found.

Cornets sound: enter the Masque, thus ordered: a torch-bearer, a shield-boy, then a masquer, so throughout; then the shield-boys fall at one end, the torch-bearers at the other; the masquers i' th' middle: the torch-bearers are the five gentlemen, the shield-boys the whores in boys' apparel; the masquers the five gallants: they bow to her; she rises and shows the like: they dance, but first deliver the shields up; she reads. The speech: their action.

KATHERINE [Reads]
"Alienis ecce crumenis!"

[**PURSENET** bows to her.

[Reads] "Fratremque patremque."

[**GOLDSTONE** bows to her.

[Reads] "Consumptio victus."

[**TAILBY** bows to her.

[Reads] "Occultos vendit honores."

[**PRIMERO** bows to her.

A cuckoo: [reads] "En avis ex avibus!"

[**FRIPPERY** bows to her.

Are you all as the speech and shields display you?

GOLDSTONE
We shall prove so.

[They go to dance, each unhasps his weapon from his side, and gives it to the torch-bearers. **KATHERINE** seems distrustful, but then **FITSGRAVE** whispers to her and falls back. At then end of which, all making an honour, **FRIPPERY** presents her with the chain of pearl.

KATHERINE
The very chain of pearl was filch'd from me!

[The **BOY** begins to sneak away.

FITSGRAVE
Hold! Stop the boy there!

[**BOY** seized. **PURSENET** stamps.

KATHERINE
Will none lay hands on him?

[**FRIPPERY** seized.

GOLDSTONE
How now?

FRIPPERY
Alas, I'm but a broker! 'Twas pawned to me in my shop.

[**FITSGRAVE, PYAMONT**, and the others discover themselves.

TAILBY
Ha, Fitsgrave!

PURSENET
Pyamont, and the rest!

GOLDSTONE
Where's Bouser?

FITSGRAVE
Here.

GOLDSTONE
We are all betrayed!

FITSGRAVE
Betrayed? You're not worthy to be to betrayed, you have not so much worth: nay, struggle not with the net, you are caught for this world.

FIRST COURTESAN
Would we were out!

FITSGRAVE
'Twas I fram'd your device, do you see? 'Twas I!
The whole assembly has took notice of it.
[To **GOLDSTONE**] That you are a gallant cheater,
So much the pawning of my cloak contains;
[to **PURSENET**] You a base thief, think of Combe Park; [to **TAILBY**] and tell me
That you're a hired smockster; here's her letter,

[to **PRIMERO**] In which we are certified that you're a bawd.

FIRST GENTLEMAN
The broker has confessed it.

SECOND GENTLEMAN
So has the boy.

TAILBY
That boy will be hanged; he stole the chain at first,
And has thus long maintained his master's gallantry

FITSGRAVE
All which we here present, like captive slaves,
Waiting that doom which their presumption craves.

KATHERINE
How easily may our suspectless sex
With fair appearing shadows be deluded!
Dear sir, you have the work so well begun,
That took from you, small glory would be won.

FITSGRAVE
Since 'tis your pleasure to refer to me
The doom of these, I have provided so,
They shall not altogether lose their cost:
See, I have brought wives for 'em.

[The **WOMEN** of the masque discover themselves.

GOLDSTONE
Heart, the strumpets! Out, out!

TAILBY
Having assum'd, out of their impudence,
The shape of shield-boys!

FRIPPERY
To heap full confusion!

FIRST COURTESAN
Rather confine us to strict chastity,
A mere impossible task, than to wed these,
Whom we do loathe worse than the foul'st disease.

GOLDSTONE
O grant 'em their requests!

FITSGRAVE
The doom is past; so, since your aim was marriage,
Either embrace it in these courtesans,
Or have your base acts and felonious lives
Proclaim'd to the indignation of the law,
Which will provide a public punishment.
As for the boy, and that infectious bawd,
We put forth those to whipping.

PRIMERO
Whipping? You find not that in the statute to whip satin.

FITSGRAVE
Away with him!

[**PRIMERO** and **BOY** led off.

GOLDSTONE
Since all our shifts are discovered, as far as I can see, 'tis our best course to marry 'em; we'll make them get our livings.

PURSENET
He says true.

MISTRESS NEWCUT
You see how we are threatened: by my troth, wenches, be ruled by me; let's marry 'em, and it be but to plague 'em; for when we have husbands we are under covert-baron, and may lie with whom we list! I have tried that in my t'other husband's days.

ALL THE COURTESANS
A match.

FITSGRAVE
I'll be no more deferr'd: come, when do you join?

GOLDSTONE
These forc'd marriages do never come to good.

FITSGRAVE
How can they when they come to such as you?

PURSENET
They often prove the ruin of great houses.

FITSGRAVE
Nor, virgin, do I in this seek to entice
All glory to myself; these gentlemen,
Whom I am bound to love for kind assistance,

Had great affinity in the plot with me.

KATHERINE
To them I give my thanks; myself to thee,
Thrice-worthy Fitsgrave!

FITSGRAVE
I have all my wishes.

KATHERINE
And I presume there's none but those can frown,
Whose envies, like the rushes, we tread down.

[Exeunt **OMMES**.

Thomas Middleton – A Short Biography

Thomas Middleton was born in London in April 1580 and baptised on 18th April. He was the son of a bricklayer who had raised himself to the status of a gentleman and become the owner of property adjoining the Curtain Theatre in Shoreditch.

Middleton was aged only five when his father died. His mother remarried but this new union unfortunately fell apart and turned into a fifteen year legal conflict centered on the inheritance of Thomas and his younger sister.

Middleton went on to attend Queen's College, Oxford, matriculating in 1598. However he failed to graduate for reasons unknown leaving either in 1600 or 1601. He had by that time written and published three long poems in popular Elizabethan styles. None appears to have been commercially successful although Microcynicon: Six Snarling Satirese was denounced by the Archbishop of Canterbury and publicly burned as part of his attack on verse satire. Although a minor work, the poems show the roots of Middleton's interest in, and later mature work on, sin, hypocrisy, and lust.

In the early years of the 17th century, Middleton made a living writing topical pamphlets, including one, Penniless Parliament of Threadbare Poets, that was reprinted several times as well as becoming the subject of a parliamentary inquiry.

For one so young he was already making quite an impact and had obviously attracted the eye of the authorities in those turbulent times.

Records surviving of the great theatrical entrepreneur of the day, Philip Henslowe, confirm that Middleton was writing for Henslowe's Admiral's Men. His lauded contemporary, a certain William Shakespeare, was writing only for Henslowe whereas Middleton remained a free agent and able to write for whichever theatrical company hired him.

These early years writing plays continued to attract controversy. His friendship and writing partnership with Thomas Dekker brought him into conflict with Ben Jonson and George Chapman in the so-called

War of the Theatres. (This controversy was also called the Poetomachia by Thomas Dekker. The Bishops Ban of 1599 had removed any use of satire from prose and verse publications and so the only outlet was on the stage. For the next 3 years Ben Jonson and George Chapman on one side and John Marston, Thomas Dekker and Thomas Middleton on the other poked fun at their opposition with characters from their plays. The grudge against Jonson continued as late as 1626, when Jonson's play The Staple of News indulges in a slur on Middleton's last play, A Game at Chess).

In 1603, Middleton married. It was also a momentous year in other respects. On the death of Elizabeth I, her cousin James VI of Scotland was now also crowned King James I of England. Another outbreak of the plague now forced the theatres in London to close.

For Middleton the changeover from Elizabethan to Jacobean was the beginning of a long period of success as a writer.

When the theatres re-opened and welcomed back audiences in need of entertainment Middleton was there, writing for several different companies. In particular he specialised in city comedy and revenge tragedy.

During this time he appears also to have written with Shakespeare and he is variously attributed as collaborating on All's Well That Ends Well and Timon of Athens.

Although Middleton had started as a junior partner to Thomas Dekker he was now his fully fledged equal. His finest work with Dekker was undoubtedly The Roaring Girl, a biography of the notorious contemporary thief Mary Frith (Frith began her criminal career as a pickpocket before moving on to highway robbery with a penchant for dressing up as a man. A spell in prison was followed by a long career as a 'fence' from her shop in Fleet St. She lived to the then quite extraordinary age of 74.) The writing is noteworthy not only for its playwriting ambition but in producing a fully formed heroine in Moll Cutpurse. This was only shortly after the role of women in plays had seen fit to have them played, in the main, by men.

In the 1610s, Middleton began another playwriting partnership, this time with the actor William Rowley, producing another slew of plays including the classics Wit at Several Weapons and A Fair Quarrel.

The ever adaptable Middleton seemed at ease working with others or by himself. His solo writing credits include the comic masterpiece, A Chaste Maid in Cheapside, in 1613. Interestingly his solo plays are somewhat less thrusting and bellicose. Certainly there is no comedy among them with the satirical depth of Michaelmas Term and no tragedy as raw, striking and as bloodthirsty as The Revenger's Tragedy.

There may be various reasons for this and among them that he was increasingly involved with civic pageants and therefore was trying to avoid too much controversy especially without the cover of a collaborator. Indeed in 1620, he was officially appointed as chronologer of the City of London, a post he held until his death in 1627, when ironically, it passed to his great rival, and sometime enemy, Ben Jonson.

Middleton's official duties did not interrupt his dramatic writing; the 1620s saw the production of his and Rowley's tragedy, and continual favourite, The Changeling, as well as several other tragicomedies.

However in 1624, he reached a peak of notoriety when his dramatic allegory A Game at Chess was staged by the King's Men. The play used the conceit of a chess game to present and satirise the recent intrigues surrounding the Spanish Match; James I's son, Prince Charles, was being positioned to marry the daughter, Maria Anna of the Spanish King Philip IV of Spain. Though Middleton's approach was strongly patriotic, the Privy Council closed the play, after only nine performances at the Globe theatre, having received a complaint from the Spanish ambassador. The Privy Council then opened a prosecution against both authors and actors. Although Middleton in his defence showed that the play had been passed by the Master of the Revels, Sir Henry Herbert, any further performance was forbidden and the author and actors fined.

What happened next is a mystery. It is the last play recorded as having being written by Middleton. His playwriting career appears to have stopped dead. It follows that some sort of further punishment probably occurred and for a writer can there be any greater punishment than not being allowed to write or be heard?

Middleton's work is diverse even by the standards of his age. His career Middleton covers many many genres including tragedy, history and city comedy. As we have noted he did not have the kind of official relationship with a particular company that Shakespeare or Fletcher had that might have supported him in a lean creative period. Instead he appears to have written on a freelance basis for any number of companies. His output ranges from the "snarling" satire of Michaelmas Term, performed by the Children of Paul's, to the bleak intrigues of The Revenger's Tragedy, performed by the King's Men. Interestingly earlier editions of The Revenger's Tragedy attributed the play solely to Cyril Tourneur but recent studies have shredded that view so that Middleton's authorship is not now seriously contested

Indeed modern techniques in analysing writing styles are now leaning towards giving Middleton credit for his adaptation and revision of Shakespeare's Macbeth and Measure for Measure. Along with the more established evidence of collaboration on All's Well That Ends Well and Timon of Athens it appears that Middleton has moved some way forward to the front rank of playwrights and an association, in some form, but its greatest exponent.

His early work was informed by the blossoming, in the late Elizabethan period, of satire, while his maturity was influenced by the ascendancy of Fletcherian tragicomedy. Middleton's later work, in which his satirical fury is tempered and broadened, includes three of his acknowledged masterpieces. A Chaste Maid in Cheapside, produced by the Lady Elizabeth's Men, which skillfully combines London life with an expansive view of the power of love to effect reconciliation even though London seems populated entirely by sinners, in which no social rank goes unsatirised. The Changeling, a later tragedy, returns Middleton to an Italianate setting like that of The Revenger's Tragedy, except that here the central characters are more fully drawn and more compelling as individuals. Similar development can be seen in Women Beware Women.

Middleton's plays are marked by their cynicism, though often very funny, about the human race. His characters are complex. True heroes are a rarity: almost all of his characters are selfish, greedy, and self-absorbed.

When Middleton does portray good people, the characters are often presented as flawless and perfect and given small, undemanding roles. A theological pamphlet attributed to Middleton gives sustenance to the notion that Middleton was a strong believer in Calvinism.

Thomas Middleton died at his home at Newington Butts in Southwark in the summer of 1627, and was buried on July 4th, in St Mary's churchyard which today survives as a public park in Elephant and Castle.

Middleton stands with John Fletcher and Ben Jonson as the most successful and prolific of playwrights from the Jacobean period. Very few Renaissance dramatists would achieve equal success in both comedy and tragedy but Middleton was one. He also wrote many masques and pageants and remains, to this day, one of the most notable of Jacobean dramatists.

Middleton's work has long been praised by many literary critics, among the most fervent were Algernon Charles Swinburne and T. S. Eliot. The latter thought Middleton was second only to Shakespeare.

Among their contemporaries was a very crowded field of talent including: Ben Jonson (1572-1637), Christopher Marlowe (1564-1593), Francis Beaumont (1585-1616), Henry Chettle (1564-1606), John Fletcher (1579–1625), John Ford (1586–1639), John Day (1574-1640), John Marston (1576-1634), John Webster (1580-1634), Nathan Field (1587-1620), Philip Massinger (1584-1640), Richard Burbage (1567-1619), Robert Greene (1558-1592), Thomas Dekker (1575-1625), Thomas Kyd (1558-1594), William Haughton (died 1605), William Rowley (1585-1626).

It's a daunting list and confirms that to top that made you a very special talent indeed.

Thomas Middleton – A Concise Bibliography

It has long been recognised that the modern concept of authorship was rather more elastic in centuries past. Writers were not only for hire, and their work therefore a commodity, but their plays ran much shorter lengths; two weeks being a common term of performance. To that themes and scenes were liberally excised from one play and used in another. Revisions to past plays that were being restaged would be undertaken and entirely credited to other writers. Many works and plays were unpublished and have not survived and some only from memory by actors etc. Whilst many of these playwrights are only now feted for their talents, some undoubtedly were at the time, but it is difficult to, in every case, to establish exact provenance. With modern scholarly and literary techniques author attributions have sometimes changed or been re-balanced. For those where this may be the case we have placed the *Play's Title and other information* in italics

Plays
Blurt, Master Constable or The Spaniard's Night Walk (with Thomas Dekker (1602)
The Phoenix (1603–4)
The Honest Whore, Part 1, a city comedy (1604), (with Thomas Dekker)
Michaelmas Term, a city comedy, (1604)
All's Well That Ends Well (1604-5); believed by some to be co-written by Middleton based on stylometric analysis.
A Trick to Catch the Old One, a city comedy (1605)
A Mad World, My Masters, a city comedy (1605)
A Yorkshire Tragedy, a one-act tragedy (1605); attributed to Shakespeare on its title page, but stylistic analysis favours Middleton.

Timon of Athens a tragedy (1605–6); stylistic analysis indicates that Middleton may have written this play in collaboration with William Shakespeare.
The Puritan (1606)
The Revenger's Tragedy (1606). Earlier editions often mistakenly attribute authorship to Cyril Tourneur.
Your Five Gallants, a city comedy (1607)
The Family of Love (1607) some attribute this to Middleton others include Dekker and Lording Barry.
The Bloody Banquet (1608–9); co-written with Thomas Dekker.
The Roaring Girl, a city comedy depicting the exploits of Mary Frith (1611); with Thomas Dekker.
No Wit, No Help Like a Woman's, a tragic-comedy (1611)
The Second Maiden's Tragedy, a tragedy (1611); an anonymous manuscript; stylistic analysis indicates Middleton's authorship (though one scholar also attributed it to Shakespeare.
A Chaste Maid in Cheapside, a city comedy (1613)
Wit at Several Weapons, a city comedy (1613); printed as part of the Beaumont and Fletcher Folio, but stylistic analysis indicates comprehensive revision by Middleton & Rowley.
More Dissemblers Besides Women, a tragicomedy (1614)
The Widow (1615–16)
The Witch, a tragicomedy (1616)
A Fair Quarrel, a tragicomedy (1616). Co-written with William Rowley.
The Old Law, a tragicomedy (1618–19). written with William Rowley and perhaps a third collaborator.
Hengist, King of Kent, or The Mayor of Quinborough, a tragedy (1620)
Women Beware Women, a tragedy (1621)
Measure for Measure (1603-4); some scholars argue that the First Folio text was partly revised by Middleton in 1621.
Anything for a Quiet Life, a city comedy (1621). Co-written with John Webster.
The Changeling, a tragedy (1622). Co-written with William Rowley.
The Nice Valour (1622). Printed as part of the Beaumont and Fletcher Folio, but stylistic analysis indicates comprehensive revision by Middleton.
The Spanish Gypsy, a tragicomedy (1623). Believed to be a play by Middleton & Rowley and later revised by Thomas Dekker and John Ford.
A Game at Chess, a political satire (1624). Satirized the negotiations over the proposed marriage of Prince Charles, son of James I of England, with the Spanish princess. Closed after nine performances.

Masques & Entertainments
The Whole Royal and Magnificent Entertainment Given to King James Through the City of London (1603–4). Co-written with Thomas Dekker, Stephen Harrison & Ben Jonson.
The Manner of his Lordship's Entertainment
The Triumphs of Truth
Civitas Amor
The Triumphs of Honour and Industry (1617)
The Masque of Heroes, or, The Inner Temple Masque (1619)
The Triumphs of Love and Antiquity (1619)
The World Tossed at Tennis (1620). Co-written with William Rowley.
Honourable Entertainments (1620–1)
An Invention (1622)
The Sun in Aries (1621)
The Triumphs of Honour and Virtue (1622)
The Triumphs of Integrity with The Triumphs of the Golden Fleece (1623)

The Triumphs of Health and Prosperity (1626)

Poetry

The Wisdom of Solomon Paraphrased (1597)
Microcynicon: Six Snarling Satires (1599)
The Ghost of Lucrece (1600)
Burbage epitaph (1619)
Bolles epitaph (1621)
Duchess of Malfi (commendatory poem) (1623)
St James (1623)
To the King (1624)

Prose

The Penniless Parliament of Threadbare Poets (1601)
News from Gravesend. Co-written with Thomas Dekker (1603)
The Nightingale and the Ant aka Father Hubbard's Tales (1604)
The Meeting of Gallants at an Ordinary (1604). Co-written with Thomas Dekker.
Plato's Cap Cast at the Year 1604 (1604)
The Black Book (1604)
Sir Robert Sherley his Entertainment in Cracovia (1609) (translation).
The Two Gates of Salvation (1609), or The Marriage of the Old and New Testament.
The Owl's Almanac (1618)
The Peacemaker (1618)

www.ingramcontent.com/pod-product-compliance
Lightning Source LLC
Chambersburg PA
CBHW061448040426
42450CB00007B/1265